The CELTIC VISION

The CELTIC VISION

Prayers, Blessings, Songs
and Invocations
from the Gaelic Tradition

Edited by Esther de Waal

Liguori/Triumph
LIGUORI, MISSOURI

Published by Liguori/Triumph
An imprint of Liguori Publications
Liguori, Missouri
www.liguori.org
www.catholicbooksonline.com

First published in 1988 as *The Celtic Vision: Prayers and Blessings from the Outer Hebrides* by Darton, Longman and Todd Ltd, London, England.

Carmina Gadelica © 1971, 1972, 1976, 1984, 1987
Trustees of Professor J. C. Watson
Introductions and selections © 1988, 2001 by Esther de Waal

Library of Congress Cataloging-in-Publication Data

Carmina gadelica. English. Selections.
    The Celtic vision : prayers, blessings, songs, and invocations from the Gaelic tradition / edited by Esther De Waal from the Carmina gadelica, orally collected in the highlands and islands of Scotland by Alexander Carmichael.
        p. cm.
    Originally published: London, England: Darton, Longman, Todd, 1988.
    ISBN 0-7648-0831-1; ISBN 0-7648-0784-6 (pbk.)
    1. Christian poetry, Scottish Gaelic—Translations into English. 2. Prayers.
I. De Waal, Esther. II. Carmichael, Alexander, 1832–1912. III. Title.

PB1684 .C37 2001
891.6'310080382—dc21   2001037752

Printed in the United States of America
05 04 03 02 01   5 4 3 2 1
Revised edition 2001

Contents

Foreword

WE HAVE WITNESSED a great deal of interest in the heritage of Celtic Christianity over the past decade. For some people it seemed to be another spiritual fad in the quickly changing scene. For others it seemed too narrow a focus and was just for the Irish or other people of Celtic background. We are, however, now seeing its staying power and its contribution to the renewal of both Church and individual believers. In my own experience of sharing insights from the Celtic tradition, I have found that when I speak and describe insights gained from the Celts I am merely articulating something already known, intuited and appreciated. The Celtic way of seeing things has come home to many people as holistic, as well grounded, and as an expression of an apt way of seeking God and reappropriating one's Christian tradition in these post-modern times. The prayers, the lives of the saints, the forms and expressions of community, and many other perspectives of Celtic Christianity strike us as so appropriate and so hopeful for today.

My own interest in Celtic Christianity began back in the nineteen-seventies when the "roots phenomenon" prompted me to start looking more deeply into my own background as an Irish-American. Thus began an ever-deepening pursuit into a culture, a civilization, a world-view and spirituality that was a surprising and delightful discovery. It proved to be something much wider than just an Irish experience. The Celtic tradition, I soon realized, embraced immediately the countries around the Irish Sea that spoke a Celtic language—Scotland, Wales, Ireland, Cornwall, Brittany and the Isle of Mann. But this tradition proved to be something even more extensive than that. The modern tools of archaeology and philology have helped us to realize that the Celtic peoples once spread over all of southern Europe and that they created a European civilization that predated and bequeathed much to the Greco-Roman civilizations that we have inherited in the west. From a religious point of view, I found that the Celtic way of seeing things also has become a source of healing and renewal to people raised with a narrower and dualistic Christian spiritual world-view. The Celtic view breaks through splits and isolations. It helps us to connect to the earth. It gives a positive perspective to us relating as male and female humans, and as human beings to all other creatures, both heavenly and earthly. With a profound awareness and belief in the Holy Trinity, it sees all relationship as inherently reflecting our being made in the image of a relation-based Triune God in whom we live and move and have our being.

Celtic Christian spirituality is in the best of our Christian tradition and brings us back to a more balanced and more richly imaginative first millennium expression of the Christian message. It is very faithful to and resonates with such Christian doctrines as that of the Triune God, Incarnation, sacramental life, communion of saints, Mystical Body of Christ. It also is very sensitive to the life of charity and social justice expressed in concern for the needy and oppressed. But, in a similar fashion common to all spiritualities, the Celtic tradition accentuates particular aspects and brings them together in a particular spirituality or even what I like to call a particular world-view. It gives us a way of seeing God, the world and one another. Having this world-view is the base of our actions and behavior. It is the base of the practical everyday way we see reality and how we live our beliefs and values.

Esther de Waal speaks in the present book of the "Celtic Vision." This is another way of speaking of the Celtic way of seeing things, a spiritual outlook on all reality. She believes this vision can renew our own Christian vision, that it can challenge our self-centered isolation and point to fellowship and unity with God and all creation. And it is Esther's gift to convey this vision to us in an exciting and challenging way. In her introductions, as well as in her editing of the prayers featured in this book, she opens this vision to us readers and entices us to listen, to respond, to see and to live.

We owe much to Esther de Waal for the current appreciation of Celtic Christianity. The original book was first published in 1988, a forerunner of many writings that introduced us to the Celtic scene in general and the value of the prayers of the *Carmina Gadelica* in particular. She had already proven herself as an insightful and prophetic writer in her making known another first millennium spirituality, that of the Rule of Saint Benedict. In the earlier eighties she had begun to write on Benedictine spirituality for lay people, an interest that continues to fascinate her. She has done a great service here for many other contemporary people as well. It strikes me as very natural that she then began to speak and write on Celtic spirituality. Her interest in Benedictine spirituality was raised when she was in residence at Canterbury Cathedral where she felt the Benedictine spirit in its very stones. Her interest in Celtic spirituality comes from her roots in living on the Welsh border and her sensing the Welsh ethos as distinct from that of the Anglo-Saxon. Both Benedictine and Celtic traditions hold much for us present-day Christians who look for spiritual guides and references to help us to move into the future with hope and inspiration. We can thank Esther de Waal for bringing these traditions to a wider audience.

The value of this present volume is in its making known to more readers the wonderful collection of poems and prayers from the *Carmina Gadelica,* five volumes of material collected and edited by Alexander Carmichael. These are intimate, imaginative expressions of people's attitudes to and reaction to the ordinary events of everyday life. They feed the religious imagination. They make us widen our sense of prayer inasmuch as they help us to pray not to just ask for things but to relate to God, the Triune God, in many ways. In her new preface to this edition of these prayers, Esther compares these prayers to the Jewish *Berakah* prayers of blessing God for all the ways in which God blesses us.

In my own ministry, I have found these prayers to be a great school and entry into the Celtic Christian mind. They enflesh the particular approaches, attitudes, and perspectives that were so richly part of the Celtic Christian's life. They reeducate our own narrower and impoverished way of praying. It was to Esther de Waal's credit that she early saw these prayers as offering so much to the contemporary spiritual seeker. This is, indeed, an older way of prayer which is new for many raised on a narrower understanding of prayer as only prayer of petition.

The first edition of this book was the outcome of the genius and beauty of these prayers combined with the insights and guidance of the author. She helped all of us to appreciate these prayers by her introduction, her notes throughout the book, and the particular prayers she chose as an editor. She omitted some prayers that would not speak to us as much today or that were more provincial and particular in interest. The prayers she chose were assembled in categories such as prayers of creation, morning and night prayers, birth and death, household prayers, journeys, Mary, Saints and Angels, Sun and Moon, and Short Blessings.

In this new edition she has added a section on prayers on plants and healing. Besides this, she has included a new preface, has rewritten the introduction, and added some new particular notes of explanation throughout the text. The result of all this is to provide readers, new and old, with a great resource. I pray it receive a wide reading. Some of us speak and write about the story and theology of Celtic Christianity and some history and reflections are needed to get back into a first millennium mind-set. But Esther de Waal has helped us to experience this spirituality in these prayers. I ask God's blessings on her and her continued work to share this rich spiritual tradition with all of us.

TIMOTHY J. JOYCE, O.S.B.
GLASTONBURY ABBEY, HINGHAM, MASSACHUSETTS

Father Timothy Joyce is the author of *Celtic Christianity: A Sacred Tradition, A Vision of Hope* (Orbis, 1998); *Celtic Quest: A Healing Journey for Irish Catholics* (Orbis, 2000).

Preface

to the Second Edition

I AM DELIGHTED to have the opportunity to write a short new preface to this book. When I first read the six volumes of the *Carmina Gadelica*, it was in the constricting circumstances of a library since the original volumes were, and are, hard to obtain. They spoke to me immediately, they touched my heart, and I wanted to make them more easily available to others like myself who might find that they brought inspiration as well as practical help in making praying a natural and unself-conscious part of daily living.

Since this book was published, there has been an extraordinary renaissance in Celtic spirituality, and there have been numbers of books of prayers based on the form of these Celtic blessings. I am sure that many people have gained immensely from this, but I feel that these original blessings, prayers, and poems still have their part to play. Perhaps the most important thing is that they take us away from the idea that prayer is essentially a matter of request and asking, asking God to bless us—our lives, our problems, our possessions—a very easy trap to fall into. Here we have something which reminds us of the Hebrew understanding of blessing: we bless the God who blesses us. So blessing becomes a reciprocal act: we are blessed by God and we bless God in return. When we do this we acknowledge God as the source of our life and the origin of all goodness and gifts. To bless is thus an act of praise and gratitude.

I am happy that I have been able to include a new short section on prayers for healing and additional blessings of food, a central and shared act of family life, as it is of the family of God in the Eucharist. In a recent book, Richard Woods reminds us: "In the end, all blessing means being close to God....For Saint Paul, every blessing flows from Christ, God's blessing itself, God's benediction on Creation, the divine presence made definitely visible and tangible. To the extent that we draw closer to Christ, the happier we become" (Richard J. Woods, *The Spirituality of the Celtic Saints*, Maryknoll, N.Y.: Orbis, 2000, p. 148). There could be no better way of expressing this justification of reissuing this volume. I hope that many people will pray with it, and beyond it, and that it may become a blessing which reminds them of how greatly we are all the recipients of the extravagant blessings of the generous outpouring of that Trinitarian God who walks the way alongside us, in the daily and the ordinary, in darkness and in light, in life and in death.

ESTHER DE WAAL
FEBRUARY 1, 2001

Preface

IN MAKING THIS SELECTION from the original six volumes of Alexander Carmichael's *Carmina Gadelica*, my aim has been to make this great treasure storehouse of Celtic spirituality more widely and easily accessible, and to present the reader with something that he or she can actually use. With this practical consideration in mind I have divided the material into categories which I hope do justice to the diversity of Carmichael's collection while making it more available and usable for readers today. This means that I have had to omit much, though not all, that is pre-Christian or semi-pagan (the charms against evil spirits and fairy songs in particular, which are ultimately more of interest to the folklorist), in order to give space to the rest. Here are hymns and blessings, poems and invocations, which are all ultimately prayers—a praying that grew out of the life itself. I hope that the short notes attached to each section will give some impression of the world which gave rise to this particular approach to prayer. It is in the belief that that way of prayer has much to give to us today that this selection is offered.

ESTHER DE WAAL

Introduction

When the people of the Isles come out in the morning to their tillage, to their fishing, to their farming, or to any of their various occupations anywhere, they say a short prayer called "Ceum na Còrach": "The Path of Right," or "The Just or True Way."[1] If the people feel secure from being overseen or overheard they croon, or sing, or intone their morning prayer in a pleasing musical manner. If, however, any person, and especially if a stranger, is seen in the way, the people hum the prayer in an inaudible undertone peculiar to themselves, like the soft murmur of the ever-murmuring sea, or like the far-distant eerie sighing of the wind among the trees, or like the muffled cadence of far-away waters, rising and falling upon the fitful autumn wind.[2]

IN THIS MOST characteristic piece of writing Alexander Carmichael brings to his readers a vivid sense not only of the people of the Outer Hebrides at prayer, but also of how close he felt the music of that prayer was to the elements themselves. In this way he is also introducing himself to us as a man who found this land and its peoples and its poetry all of a unity. A lifetime spent in collecting was also a lifetime spent in friendship with its people and a deep feeling for its natural beauty, as well as knowledge of its dangers and some of its dark secrets.

Alexander Carmichael was born on December 1, 1832, in the island of Lismore, where his family farmed. His first hope had been to go into the army but the death of his father changed this, and instead he accepted a nomination for the civil service. He had received his education at the Greenock Academy and at a collegiate school in Edinburgh. Working in excise gave him the chance to live in many parts of the Highlands and Islands. From his boyhood he had shown an interest in local antiquities and folklore, but it was in Uist that he was to develop this so significantly. He was there in the years before the Education Act of 1872 began the final corruption of the Gaelic oral tradition, and he was able to take advantage of his time among them to get to know the local inhabitants really well. His official life was to take him to Skye, Oban, Uist for a second time, and Edinburgh. His collecting—his lifetime passion—was to take him throughout the Isles so that he came to know them intimately. The greater part of his collection was made in the Western Isles, otherwise the Outer Hebrides, or Outer Isles, a series of islands lying beyond Skye off the northwest coast of Scotland. This long chain runs for 125 miles like a huge artificial kite stretched out along the Atlantic, with immense stretches of bleak and barren, treeless and rocky, terrain. "No mind could conceive, no imagination could realize, the disorderly distribution of land and water that is to be seen in those Outer Islands," he wrote, "where mountain and moor, sand and peat, rock and morass, reef and shoal, fresh-water lake and salt-water loch, in wildest confusion strive for mastery."[3]

In January 1868, when he was stationed in North Uist, Alexander Carmichael married Mary Francis MacBean, and in 1882, they removed permanently to Edinburgh. She would sometimes accompany her husband on his frequent and often prolonged visits to the Isles, but her real support lay in her good management which enabled him to bear the financial strain of his adventures and to wander about as the spirit moved him. For sixty years he was able to pursue his Gaelic pilgrimages. Year in, year out, he devoted himself to his self-imposed task. He traveled incessantly, and even in his late seventies was tackling journeys that would have defeated lesser men. His physical stamina must have been extraordinary. His adventures by ford and ferry in the Outer Hebrides became proverbial. On land he avoided the highway whenever possible and set out across the wilds, walking long distances on sheep tracks and bridle paths. More than once, after a long journey through peat-hags and corries, he would spend the night on a hard chair in front of the fire in a shepherd's hut.

The *Carmina Gadelica* was the fruit of those travels. It came out of a world that was full of song and music, whether private and secret, or communal and shared. "The people of that day were full of hymns and prayers, full of music and songs, full of joy and melody and innocent merriment," as one reciter, Catherine Macphee of Uist, told him. "By the Book itself, you would not ask but to be hearing them…however wild the weather, however miry the road, however dark the night going homeward. That was our school, and we had no other."[4] Music and song was part of their working time and of their leisure. Those who had worked together during the day met in the evenings, crowding into one another's houses, as one of them described it to Alexander Carmichael, "telling tales and histories, invocations and prayers, singing hymns and songs, runes and lays, sweet, beautiful and soft."[5] These were of course the *"ceilidh,"* times of entertainment with storytelling, heroic ballads, tales often long enough to occupy several nights.

But Alexander Carmichael was not concerned with the public and the heroic. He would visit men and women in their own homes, spend long hours with them, listening while they intoned in a low, recitative manner and their voices rose and fell in slow modulated cadences, sounds which reminded him of the moaning of the waves or the sighing of the wind on the seashore. Mary Gillies was one of those, whom despite her sufferings from age and illness he found still a beautiful woman. Unlettered, like most of her fellow crofters, but generous and hospitable, she was ready to share both "her limited food and her unlimited lore."[6] He took from her the magnificent prayer which opens this anthology, and listening he felt that here "music and poetry and pleasure" all flowed together.

It was undoubtedly the sympathy and warmth of his approach

which enabled him to break down the natural reticence of these people and to obtain so much material that they would never otherwise have divulged to an outsider. His love for them, and for their ways, convinced them that he was not merely collecting and dissecting their beliefs in the name of science. "We thought of him rather as one who saw with our eyes, who felt with our heart, and who reproduced our past because he loved it himself and was proud of it."[7] This trust certainly helped him considerably. He never let his passionate search for whatever he had set his heart on unearthing override his warm human understanding of the men and women from whom he was collecting. A friend tells how one reciter, who gave Carmichael a singularly beautiful going-to-sleep rune, returned the next morning, having traveled twenty-six miles, to exact a pledge that his "little prayer" should never be allowed to appear in print. "Think ye," said the old man, "if I slept a wink last night for thinking of what I had given away. Proud, indeed, shall I be, if it give pleasure to yourself, but I should not like cold eyes to read it in a book."[8] So while others might have been given the heroic tales and ballads which were recited in public at the *"ceilidh,"* Carmichael was privileged to hear "the things which were said when the door was closed, and the lights were out."

They gave him the prayers whose daily and yearly rhythms marked their lives: prayers from birth to death, from dawn to dusk, from the start of the year until its close, for they lived quite naturally in a state of prayer. It was a praying which responded to, and grew out of, their way of life, not one imposed from outside it by an institutional church, even though most of them were Roman Catholics. (Carmichael noted in passing, however, that although these prayers had been rescued chiefly from among the Roman Catholics and in the islands, they were equally common among Protestants and on the mainland.)[9]

What they said and sung—for these prayers were also hymns and poetry, the two cannot be separated—grew out of their sense of the presence of God as the most immediate reality in their lives. Religion permeated everything they did. They made no distinction between the secular and the sacred. They were unable to discern boundaries of where religion began and ended and thus found it natural to assume that God was lovingly concerned in everything they did. They felt totally at home with God.

Carmichael was struck on going into their houses to hear how they addressed the "great God of life, the Father of all living. They press upon Him their needs and their desires fully and familiarly, but with all the awe and deference due to the Great Chief whom they wish to approach and to attract….And all this in language so homely yet so eloquent, so simple and yet so dignified, that the impressiveness could not be greater."[10] Catherine Maclennan told him:

> My mother would be asking us to sing our morning song to God down in the back-house, as Mary's lark was singing it up in the clouds and as Christ's mavis was singing it yonder in the tree, giving glory to the God of the creatures for the repose of the night, for the light of the day, and for the joy of life. She would tell us that every creature on the earth here below and in the ocean beneath and in the air above was giving glory to the great God of the creatures and the worlds, of the virtues and the blessings, and would *we* be dumb![11]

This was how the children were taught to start each day. It told them that they were part of the worship of the whole world. Again and again the *Carmina Gadelica* echo this sense of completeness which sees men and women in the context of the whole universe, and ends with the integration of the person, body and soul, heart and mind.[12] As she gave him the prayer "Bless to me, O God," Catherine Maclennan added, "My mother taught us what we should ask for in the prayer, as she heard it from her own mother, and as she again heard it from the one who was before her."[13]

In these pages we meet the men and women who would otherwise remain without name or memory. Anne Campbell he tells us was a bright, beautiful women and a sweet singer full of "songs and ballads, tales and traditions, as were her father and mother. She learned these when she was "a poor little toddling child on the knee of my mother," and then Carmichael adds: "Her mother's songs and stories, like those of all Highland mothers, were about hosts and fairies, birds and beasts, seals and fishes, and about what all these said to one another before the sins of man rendered them speechless."[14] It is the unity, the interconnectedness of this world which strikes us all the time—they belonged to a dynamic universe. Perhaps today, with the language of the new science and of the Internet we are in a better position to find resonance in what they are saying about the totality of life rather than the mechanistic approach which had earlier colored our understanding.

Here are seen a people who move easily between worlds, the seen and the unseen, the Christian and the pre-Christian. They encounter fairies and hold conversations with them but they also walk at ease with the members of the Trinity. Mary Macrae was a dairy woman in Harris who even at the age of ninety-nine would walk to church every Sunday. One stormy day of wind and snow the minister expected no one to come but all the same went down to the church and found her there: "Mary, Mary, what has brought you out on such a day and all alone?" When she said that she was not alone and he glanced round the empty church she replied: "I am not alone at all; far from it. There were three dear and loved friends with me every step of the road coming…three dear kind friends, the Father, the Son, and the Spirit were with me every step of the way."[15]

They were equally aware of the presence of the fairies, and they feared them. "The fairies are little, lovely, daring, dignified creatures, with green raiment. If they get an inch they will take an ell, and there is no gainsaying them." They were particularly keen to seize small nursing babies and had to be outwitted with a quick response. Here is the ending of a dialogue between a mortal woman nursing a child and a fairy woman who stood before them stubbornly, stiffly, starkly, peering, staring the baby straight in the face.

"White is the skin of thy child, woman,"
    said the fairy woman.
"White of skin is the snow of the peaks,"
    said the nurse.
"Pretty and golden are thy child's locks, woman,"
    said the fairy woman.
"Pretty and golden is the daisy of the plain,"
    said the nurse.
"Sharp and cutting is thy tongue,"
    said the fairy woman,
"It was never set to a grindstone," said the nurse.

When she saw that the mortal would not yield an inch, the fairy woman turned the back of her head and departed by the way she had come. The woman, obviously admiring some quality of strength and determination that she saw in the fairy, went on to speak of a wren, a bird whom she clearly admires but with whom she has a very different relationship:

Think of the wren himself, how brash and bold he comes and sits on the window sill until I give him food. When he gets the food he make his bob to me and is off, and I see neither the black nor the white of him until he grows hungry again, or until bad weather and hard times and scarcity of food come, and he brings one or two of his numerous little family to me in search of food. The poor creature lives but from hour to hour, from hand to mouth, from day to day, as I do myself. It is a matter for thought, the work of creation and the goodness of the great God of the elements to His creatures, great and small; and I! I! I am one of them![16]

Children learned from their earliest years to be aware of the fullness of life in the natural world around them. A mother will sing her child to sleep with a long lullaby (and repetition is part of the strength of the oral tradition) in which she tells of all the differing nesting places of the birds as she nestles her own child in her arms. Of the twenty-five verses, here are a few:

> The nest of the wren
> Is in the rock thicket,
>> My little one will sleep and he shall have the bird.

> The nest of the raven
> Is in the hawthorn rock,
>> My little one will sleep and he shall have the bird.

> The nest of the blackbird
> Is in the withered bough,
>> My little one will sleep and he shall have the bird.

> The nest of the cuckoo
> Is in the hedge-sparrow's nest,
>> My little one will sleep and he shall have the bird.

> The nest of the kite
> Is high on the mountain-slope,
>> My little one will sleep and he shall have the bird.[17]

The woman singing at their work had many songs, which they sang alone or together. The shared task of the making of cloth gave one of the best opportunities for singing about everything under the sun, stories of the past, heroic legends, songs of the seas and of the hills, of battles and cursings and death. But also the gentle songs which grew out of their sense of connectedness with the natural world:

> O apple tree, apple branch,
>> O apple tree o ho,
> Apple tree, flourishing apple tree,
>> O apple tree o ho.

O apple tree, may God be with thee,
May moon and sun be with thee,
May the east and west winds be with thee,
May the great Creator of the elements be with thee,
May everything that ever existed be with thee.[18]

All that Alexander Carmichael collected had in fact been handed down from generation to generation. Since much material was transcribed in the 1860s from people who were then old and who had heard it in their childhood from those who were already old themselves, this would carry it back to the first half of the seventeenth century. Carmichael himself preferred to leave the question of historical roots to conjecture. "It is the product of far-away thinking, come down on the long stream of time. Who the thinkers and whence the stream, who can tell?" he asked.[19] He went on to suggest, rather romantically, that the ultimate origins of these hymns lay in the monastic cells of Derry or Iona, but this of course cannot be established historically.

Yet he is surely right in suggesting that the *Carmina Gadelica* should be seen as part of the wider Celtic tradition, with its particular vision of God and of the world of his creating. One of the earliest expressions of that is, of course, Saint Patrick's breastplate, which confronts us with a tremendous affirmative statement about the creator.

I arise today
Through a mighty strength, the invocation
    of the Trinity,
Through belief in the threeness,
Through confession of the oneness
Of the Creator of Creation.

As the great litany continues—and that it clearly owes much to pre-Christian origins does nothing to diminish its power—the Creator is seen in and through the world of his creating.

I arise today
Through strength of heaven
Light of sun,
Radiance of moon,
Splendor of fire,
Speed of lightning,
Swiftness of wind,
Depth of sea,
Stability of earth,
Firmness of rock.

Until finally it becomes:

Christ with me, Christ before me, Christ behind me,
Christ in me, Christ beneath me, Christ above me.[20]

The foundation stone of such an outlook is simply that this is God's world, that creation is good, and that material things reflect their creator. Perhaps because they were converted to Christianity very early the Irish received the Gospel at a time when the church was sure that the goodness of God healed and restored the whole of creation. This theme of common creation is found as much in an eighth-century Irish hermit writing in his hut in the woods as it is in a twentieth-century Welsh poet. Everything that surrounds him, each color and sound speak to him of Christ.

A tree of apples of great bounty like a mansion, stout: a pretty bush, thick as a fist, of small hazel-nuts, branching and green....The sound of the wind against a branching wood, grey cloud, riverfalls, the cry of the swan, delightful music![21]

Here is a world "charged with the grandeur of God," in the familiar words of Gerard Manley Hopkins. It is also here that a modern Welsh poet, Euros Bowen, stands. He writes of how the reredos of clear glass in the church draws his attention from the communion table to the world outside, to the "green blueness of the earth."

> And I noticed
> The priest's eyes
> As if he were unknowingly
> Putting his hands
> On these gifts,
> As if these gifts of nature
> Were
> The bread and the wine.[22]

The prayers of the Outer Hebrides constantly find the presence of God in and through such "gifts of nature."

> There is no plant in the ground
> But it is full of His virtue,
> There is no form in the strand
> But it is full of His blessing....
>
> There is no bird on the wing,
> There is no star in the sky,
> There is nothing beneath the sun,
> But proclaims His goodness.[23]

This is no sentimental or romantic pantheism. It is a recognition that everything good comes from God, to be enjoyed for itself and as a reflection of its creator and giver.

The nearness of God to his creation brought a strong sense that the heavenly powers were not far away but surrounded men and women day and night. It seemed natural to them to turn to the Trinity and to Mary, to the saints and angels, for support and for practical aid in everything that happened in their lives. Getting dressed and lighting the fire, milking the cows and making butter, grinding the meal and weaving the cloth, driving the flocks to the fields, and fishing, sowing the seed and harvesting the grain—all these become the occasion for praying and for involving the heavenly powers. That simple phrase of a prayer "Bless the handling of my hands" expresses a desire to consecrate each thing they did to God. There is no divide here between this world and the next. Heaven and earth are interconnected and interacting. So Mary is there at the start of the day when the peats have to be lifted from the hearth. Saint Bridget will help with the making of the butter. Gabriel and the angels can be summoned for the sowing of the seed. Saint Columba will protect the cattle on the way to the fields. There are prayers and poems for each labor of the day and for each event in the passing year. Perhaps the milking croons, which the woman sang quietly as she milked her cows, show better than any others how completely at ease she felt with the saints, how free to ask for that most practical piece of help, holding the cow still.

> Come, Mary, and milk my cow,
> Come, Bride, and encompass her,
> Come, Columba the benign,
>   And twine thine arms around my cow....
>
> Come, Mary Virgin, to my cow,
> Come, great Bride, the beauteous,
> Come, thou milkmaid of Jesus Christ,
>   And place thine arms beneath my cow.[24]

This awareness of being surrounded by heavenly forces, which began at dawn, continued throughout the day until it was time for sleep. Then they could commend the hours of darkness to God, knowing that saints and angels were here too.

> I lie down tonight
> With fair Mary and with her Son,
> With pure-white Michael,
> And with Bride beneath her mantle.[25]

The saints and angels are never remote.

> I see angels on clouds
> Coming with speech and friendship to us.[26]

The saints are equally familiar. Perhaps because they were known through legend to be able to combine miraculous powers with human foibles, Celtic saints were felt to be more approachable. Saint Bridget of course was extremely popular and women felt close to another woman who would help them, particularly at child-birth.[27]

> Brigit is my companion-woman,
> Brigit is my maker of song,
> Brigit is my helping-woman,
> My choicest of women,
> my woman of guidance.[28]

Even the apostles show a human face. Peter is not the man with the keys but the man of "sleep and of fear." But, above all, Mary, while still hailed as the Queen of Heaven, is also a woman to whom to confide about duties around the house, a woman who knew their sort of life since she herself had experienced simplicity, hardship, and tears.

> That gives unto me
> The hope excelling
> That my tears and my prayer
> May find guest-room with thee.[29]

So when death comes they know that the saints will be waiting with arms stretched out. The tenderness of this blessing speaks for itself.

> Be each saint in heaven,
> Each sainted woman in heaven,
> Each angel in heaven
> Stretching their arms for you,
> Smoothing the way for you,
> When you go thither
>> Over the river hard to see.[30]

Perhaps it is in their seeing God as Trinity that this warmth and sense of constant presence is most forcibly expressed.

> I am bending my knee
> In the eye of the Father who created me,
> In the eye of the Son who purchased me,
> In the eye of the Spirit who cleansed me,
>> In friendship and affection.[31]

This is the triune God who is claimed in "friendliness and love." But then Hebridean life actually started with a commitment to the Trinity. Immediately after birth, in a ceremony that preceded that of baptism in church, the child would be sprinkled by the aid-woman with three drops on its forehead in the name of the Trinity, and the mother would quietly whisper

> The blessing of the Holy Three
> Little love, be dower to thee,
> Wisdom, Peace and Purity.[32]

Throughout the rest of life the Trinity will be sought in blessings which ask for the various gifts associated with each member, so that the three together may help to bring fullness of life.

> I send witness to Father,
>> Who formed all flesh;
> I send witness to Christ,
>> Who suffered scorn and pain;

> I send witness to Spirit,
>   Who will heal my wound,
> Who will make me as white
>   As the cotton-grass of the moor.[33]

Invocations for guidance and for protection are endless, so powerfully is the presence of the Trinity felt.

> The Three Who are over me,
> The Three Who are below me,
> The Three Who are above me here,
> The Three Who are above me yonder;
> The Three Who are in the earth,
> The Three Who are in the air,
> The Three Who are in the heaven,
>   The Three Who are in the great pouring sea.[34]

This of course has many affinities with the Irish breastplate prayers. It is also interesting to find an echo in a seventeenth-century Welsh writer Morgan Llwyd: "The Trinity abides with us exactly the same as the ore in the earth, or a man in his house, or a child in the womb, or a fire in a stove, or the sea in a well, or as the soul is in the eye, so is the Trinity in the godly."[35]

The prominence given to the Trinity conveys to us something of how these men and women felt about themselves and their world. A God who is Trinity in unity challenges self-centered isolation and points instead to fellowship. Or it might be better to put it another way, to say that in a society in which household, family, and kin were central realities perhaps men and women felt themselves at home with a Godhead whose very essence was a harmonious relationship of persons. This sense of relationship however was not simply to the Godhead and to human persons. It embraced the whole of creation. The keynote here is a sense of unity. It starts with a people who feel at unity with themselves—caught in that small but significant phrase "O bless myself entire"—and then this sense of unity grows outwards, to include family and kin, to birds and animals, to material things, to the whole of creation.

> Bless to me, O God, the moon that is above me,
> Bless to me, O God, the earth that is beneath me,
> Bless to me, O God, my wife and my children,
> And bless, O God, myself who have the care of them.[36]

God is at work making his world whole. That in sum is the message of the *Carmina Gadelica*. Everything, internal and external, is under the sway of God. But we should not be tempted to think that this comes from some idyllic world close to the garden of Eden. There is a danger that the reader today might imagine that these prayers and poems reflect a pastoral way of life of complete freedom and simplicity. Nothing could be further from the truth. Life was harsh and relentlessly demanding, particularly for those engaged in crofting,[37] even though its smallness of scale brought some compensations. Perhaps we can appreciate the strength of what they were saying if we look with the same eye at the ugly and heavily industrialized areas of today. Then we can recognize that it is still possible to let the ordinary and the mundane be transformed. A contemporary Welsh poet can find signs in the valleys of South Wales of the all-encompassing mystery of God. If his writing jolts us into "seeing" how God breaks through poverty and greyness then we are touched by the same vision that allowed men and women in the Outer Hebrides to see and to feel God in a life that must often have been hard and cruel. Here Gwenallt is writing about how the racing pigeons, who are "doves" in Welsh, return home from distant beauty to the grey valleys from which they started.

> They would circle about in the smoke-filled sky
>   Giving color to the twisted gloom;
> Lumps of beauty in the midst of the haze;
>   The Holy Ghost's image above the Cwm.

The Holy Ghost sanctifying the smoke,
    Turning worker to person of flesh and blood,
The cash nexus transformed in the order of grace
    And the Unions part of the household of God.[38]

In the Hebrides they felt themselves surrounded with a sky "made white by angels' wings." But the vision is the same.

Perhaps even more telling is the Celtic gift which can find the presence of God in the safe and unquestioned routine of an ordinary family day, so that occasions taken for granted become instead occasions for finding God. Again it is a question of vision, and again a vision which is still possible today, as another contemporary Welsh poet reminds us. Bobbi Jones shows us his family round the tea table:

There's something religious in the way we sit
At the tea table, a tidy family of three.
You, my love, slicing the bread and butter, and she,
The red-cheeked tot a smear of blackberry jam,
    and me....
A new creation is established, a true presence.
And talking to each other, breaking words over food
Is somehow different from customary chatting.[39]

This is after all nothing more than a modern example of the Hebridean domestic activity which became the opportunity for God breaking in on the ordinary and the familiar. It depends entirely on how we choose to see.

This I believe is what the *Carmina Gadelica* can bring to us today. It can renew our vision. These prayers can help us to see as the men and women from whom Alexander Carmichael collected them saw: to see creation and God the creator in and through that creation; to see the material things which they handled in their daily lives as a way to God; to see beyond this world to the next so that the barriers go down between earth and heaven. Here is something as true in a tower-block or a suburban house as in a crofter's cottage. As we listen to these men and women and watch them in their daily lives it would be hard to imagine a more down-to-earth spirituality than theirs. Because they found that God penetrates, informs, and consecrates the temporal order they also found that that temporal order carries a deep sense of mystery, a sense of what lies beyond. It is an irony that while our actual universe has grown so much more accessible, and mass communications have opened up so many new horizons, our inner world has in fact in some ways contracted, our inner horizons have become narrower. We find that we have lost the awareness and sensitivity possessed by a people who probably never left home in their lives. Yet to read the *Carmina Gadelica* is not merely to be transported back into a vanished world. It is to be given a vision of a world which still lies to hand, a gift waiting for us if we should choose to take it.

Source references, in the notes and following each extract, to volume and page of the *Carmina Gadelica* are given in roman and arabic numbers, for example III, 49 in note 1 below. *Italicized page numbers* refer *to pages in this book.*

1. III, 49; *p. 86.*
2. III, 48–9.
3. I, xxvi.
4. III, 351.
5. III, 21.
6. III, 40–1.
7. Rev. Dr. Kenneth MacLeod, "Our Interpreter," IV, xxix.
8. Ibid., xxxi.
9. I, xl.
10. I, 67.
11. III, 25.
12. See "I believe, O God of all gods" (III, 41; *p. 1)* which opens this anthology and which was originally intended as a morning prayer.
13. III, 25; see *p. 14.*
14. V, 228–9
15. V, 168–9
16. V, 237

17. v, 369–71.

18. v, 7.

19. I, xl.

20. This is Kuno Meyer's translation, taken from *Selections from Ancient Irish Poetry* (London, Constable, 1911).

21. Gerard Murphy (ed.), *Early Irish Lyrics, Eighth to Twelfth Century* (Oxford: Oxford University Press, 1956), p. II.

22. Euros Bowen, b. 1904–1988. From his *Detholion* (Cardiff, Yr Academi Cymreig, 1984), p. 199. I owe this translation to the Rev. James Coutts.

23. I, 39–41; *p. 5*.

24. I, 271; *p. 44*.

25. I, 81; *p. 55*.

26. I, 13–9.

27. See *pp. 130–2*.

28. III, 163; *p. 133*.

29. III, 119.

30. III, 203; *p. 133*.

31. I, 3; *p. 7*.

32. See *pp. 61–2*.

33. III, 137.

34. III, 93.

35. T. E. Ellis and J. H. Davies, *Gweithiau Morgan Llwyd* (Bangor, University of Wales Press, 1899), vol. I, p. 188. I owe this reference to the Rev. Saunders Davies.

36. III, 339; *p. 8*.

37. See James Hunter, *The Making of the Crofting Community* (Edinburgh, John Donald, 1976).

38. D. Gwenallt Jones, *Eples* (Llandysul, Gomer Press, 1951), p. 39. Translated Joseph P. Clancy, *Twentieth-Century Welsh Poems* (Llandysul, Gomer Press, 1982), p. 99. A cwm is a valley.

39. Bobbi Jones, *Selected Poems,* translated Joseph P. Clancy (Swansea, Christopher Davies, 1987), p. 63. I owe this reference to the Rev. Canon A. M. Allchin.

The
CELTIC VISION

Creation

THERE IS LITTLE TO ADD about this section which has not been said already in the Introduction. These prayers and poems bring a powerful sense of the unity of the whole created order, God and the universe, saints and angels, men and women—and not least the unity within each individual person. Underlying is a deep sense of gratitude that everything comes from God. Here in these credal hymns and litanies are some of the most magnificent celebrations of God as creator.

I Am Giving Thee Worship
With My Whole Life

I believe, O God of all gods,
 That Thou art the eternal Father of life;
I believe, O God of all gods,
 That Thou art the eternal Father of love.

I believe, O God of all gods,
 That Thou art the eternal Father of the saints;
I believe, O God of all gods,
 That Thou art the eternal Father of each one.

I believe, O God of all gods,
    That Thou art the eternal Father of mankind;
I believe, O God of all gods,
    That Thou art the eternal Father of the world.

I believe, O Lord and God of the peoples,
That Thou art the creator of the high heavens,
That Thou art the creator of the skies above,
That Thou art the creator of the oceans below.

I believe, O Lord and God of the peoples,
    That Thou art He Who created my soul and
        set its warp,

Who created my body from dust and from ashes,
    Who gave to my body breath,
        and to my soul its possession.

        Father, bless to me my body,
        Father, bless to me my soul,
        Father, bless to me my life,
        Father, bless to me my belief.

Father eternal and Lord of the peoples,
    I believe that Thou hast remedied my soul in the Spirit
        of healing,
That Thou gavest Thy loved Son in covenant for me,
That Thou has purchased my soul with the precious blood
    of Thy Son.

Father eternal and Lord of life,
    I believe that Thou didst pour on me the Spirit of grace
        at the bestowal of baptism.

· · · · ·

Father eternal and Lord of mankind,
Enwrap Thou my body and my soul beloved,
Safeguard me this night in the sanctuary of Thy love,
Shelter me this night in the shelter of the saints.

Thou hast brought me up from last night
To the gracious light of this day,
Great joy to provide for my soul,
And to do excelling good to me.

Thanks be to Thee, Jesu Christ,
     For the many gifts Thou hast bestowed on me,
Each day and night, each sea and land,
     Each weather fair, each calm, each wild.

I am giving Thee worship with my whole life,
     I am giving Thee assent with my whole power,
I am giving Thee praise with my whole tongue,
     I am giving Thee honor with my whole utterance.

I am giving Thee reverence with my whole understanding,
     I am giving Thee offering with my whole thought,
I am giving Thee praise with my whole fervor,
     I am giving Thee humility in the blood of the Lamb.

I am giving Thee love with my whole devotion,
     I am giving Thee kneeling with my whole desire,
I am giving Thee love with my whole heart,
     I am giving Thee affection with my whole sense;
I am giving Thee my existence with my whole mind,
     I am giving Thee my soul, O God of all gods.

My thought, my deed,
 My word, my will,
My understanding, my intellect,
 My way, my state.

I am beseeching Thee
To keep me from ill,
To keep me from hurt,
To keep me from harm;

To keep me from mischance,
To keep me from grief,
To keep me this night
 In the nearness of Thy love.

May God shield me,
May God fill me,
May God keep me,
May God watch me.

May God bring me
 To the land of peace,
 To the country of the King,
  To the peace of eternity.

Praise to the Father,
Praise to the Son,
Praise to the Spirit,
 The Three in One.

III, 41—7

Jesu Who Ought to Be Praised

It were as easy for Jesu
To renew the withered tree
As to wither the new
Were it His will so to do.
    Jesu! Jesu! Jesu!
    Jesu! meet it were to praise Him.

There is no plant in the ground
But is full of His virtue,
There is no form in the strand
But is full of His blessing.
    Jesu! Jesu! Jesu!
    Jesu! meet it were to praise Him.

There is no life in the sea,
There is no creature in the river,
There is naught in the firmament,
But proclaims His goodness.
    Jesu! Jesu! Jesu!
    Jesu! meet it were to praise Him.

There is no bird on the wing,
There is no star in the sky,
There is nothing beneath the sun,
But proclaims His goodness.
    Jesu! Jesu! Jesu!
    Jesu! meet it were to praise Him.

I, 39–41

Bless to Me, O God

Bless to me, O God,
    Each thing mine eye sees;
Bless to me, O God,
    Each sound mine ear hears;
Bless to me, O God,
    Each odor that goes to my nostrils;
Bless to me, O God,
    Each taste that goes to my lips;
    Each note that goes to my song,
    Each ray that guides my way,
    Each thing that I pursue,
    Each lure that tempts my will,
    The zeal that seeks my living soul,
The Three that seek my heart,
    The zeal that seeks my living soul,
The Three that seek my heart.

III, 33

I Am Bending My Knee

I am bending my knee
In the eye of the Father who created me,
In the eye of the Son who purchased me,
In the eye of the Spirit who cleansed me,
 In friendship and affection.
Through Thine own Anointed One, O God,
Bestow upon us fullness in our need.
 Love towards God,
 The affection of God,
 The smile of God,
 The wisdom of God,
 The grace of God,
 The fear of God,
 And the will of God
To do on the world of the Three,
As angels and saints
Do in heaven;
 Each shade and light,
 Each day and night,
 Each time in kindness,
 Give Thou us Thy Spirit.

I, 3

Thou God of Life

Bless to me, O God, the moon that is above me,
Bless to me, O God, the earth that is beneath me,
Bless to me, O God, my wife and my children,
And bless, O God, myself who have care of them;
    Bless to me my wife and my children,
      And bless, O God, myself who have care of them.

Bless, O God, the thing on which mine eye doth rest,
Bless, O God, the thing on which my hope doth rest,
Bless, O God, my reason and my purpose,
Bless, O bless Thou them, Thou God of life;
    Bless, O God, my reason and my purpose,
      Bless, O bless Thou them, Thou God of life.

Bless to me the bed-companion of my love,
Bless to me the handling of my hands,
Bless, O bless Thou to me, O God,
      the fencing of my defense,
And bless, O bless to me the angeling of my rest;
    Bless, O bless Thou to me, O God,
      the fencing of my defense,
And bless, O bless to me the angeling of my rest.

III, 339

My God and My Chief

My God and my Chief,
    I seek to Thee in the morning,
My God and my Chief,
    I seek to Thee this night.
I am giving Thee my mind,
    I am giving Thee my will,
I am giving Thee my wish,
    My soul everlasting and my body.

Mayest Thou be chieftain over me,
    Mayest Thou be master unto me,
Mayest Thou be shepherd over me,
    Mayest Thou be guardian unto me,
Mayest Thou be herdsman over me,
    Mayest Thou be guide unto me,
Mayest Thou be with me, O Chief of chiefs,
    Father everlasting and God of the heavens.

III, 347

Gently and Generously

Pray I this day my prayer to Thee, O God,
Voice I this day as voices the voice of Thy mouth,
Keep I this day as keep the people of heaven,
Spend I this day as spend Thine own household,

Go I this day according to Thy laws, O God,
Pass I this day as pass the saints in heaven.

Thou loving Christ Who wast hanged upon the tree,
Each day and each night remember I Thy covenant;
In my lying down and rising up I yield me to Thy cross,
In my life and my death my health Thou art and my peace.

Each day may I remember the sources of the mercies
    Thou hast bestowed on me gently and generously;
Each day may I be fuller in love to Thyself.

. . . . .

Each thing I have received from Thee it came,
Each thing for which I hope, from Thy love it will come,
Each thing I enjoy, it is of Thy bounty,
Each thing I ask, comes of Thy disposing.

Holy God, loving Father, of the word everlasting,
Grant me to have of Thee this living prayer:
Lighten my understanding, kindle my will, begin my doing,
Incite my love, strengthen my weakness, enfold my desire.

Cleanse my heart, make holy my soul, confirm my faith,
Keep safe my mind and compass my body about;
As I utter my prayer from my mouth,
In mine own heart may I feel Thy presence.

And do Thou grant, O God of life,
That Thou be at my breast, that Thou be at my back,
That Thou give me my needs as may befit the crown
    Thou hast promised to us in the world beyond.

And grant Thou to me, Father beloved,
From Whom each thing that is freely flows,
That no tie over-strict, no tie over-dear
    May be between myself and this world below.

    Place I in Thee my hope, O God,
    My living hope in the Father of the heavens,
    My great hope to be with Thyself
      In the distant world to come.

    Father and Son and Spirit,
      The One Person of the Three,
    Perfect, world without end,
      Changeless through life eternal.

III, 59–61

My Life and My Creed

Father, bless me in my body,
    Father, bless me in my soul;
Father, bless me this night
    In my body and in my soul.

Father, bless me in my life,
    Father, bless me in my creed;
Father, bless me in my tie
    To my life and to my creed.

Father, sanctify to me my speech,
    Father, sanctify to me my heart;
Father, sanctify to me every whit
    In my speech and in my heart.

    III, 349

Chief of Chiefs

God with me lying down,
God with me rising up,
God with me in each ray of light,
Nor I a ray of joy without Him,
    Nor one ray without Him.

Christ with me sleeping,
Christ with me waking,
Christ with me watching,
Every day and night,
    Each day and night.

God with me protecting,
The Lord with me directing,
The Spirit with me strengthening,
For ever and for evermore,
    Ever and evermore, Amen.
      Chief of chiefs, Amen.

    I, 5

Morning Prayers

"IF WE WERE DILATORY in putting on our clothes, and made an excuse for our prayers, my mother would say that God regarded heart and not speech, the mind and not the manner; and that we might clothe our souls with grace while clothing our bodies with raiment," said Catherine Maclennan[1] as she gave Alexander Carmichael the prayer at dressing which appears on pages 14–15.[2] These morning prayers naturally ask for a blessing on the persons themselves, the whole self commended to God in all its aspects, and not least the "handling of my hand" for the day of work which lay ahead for all, except small children. These were really morning hymns, a "tune of music" to establish the right context for the rest of the day. They were always sung, crooned or intoned. "When they would arise in the morning—and Mary mild, early-rising and early astir were the people of that day!—there could always be heard a man here and a woman there, a lad yonder and a maiden at hand, with a cheerful strain of music in the mouth of each."[3]

1. III, 25.
2. *p. 14–5.*
3. III, 35.

Prayer at Rising

Thou King of moon and sun,
  Thou King of stars beloved,
Thou Thyself knowest our need,
  O Thou merciful God of life.

Each day that we move,
  Each time that we awaken,
Causing vexation and gloom
  To the King of hosts Who loved us.

Be with us through each day,
  Be with us through each night;
Be with us each night and day,
  Be with us each day and night.

III, 29

Prayer at Dressing

Bless to me, O God,
  My soul and my body;
Bless to me, O God,
  My belief and my condition;

Bless to me, O God,
  My heart and my speech,
And bless to me, O God,
  The handling of my hand;

Strength and busyness of morning,
Habit and temper of modesty,
Force and wisdom of thought,
And Thine own path, O God of virtues,
    Till I go to sleep this night;

Thine own path, O God of virtues,
    Till I go to sleep this night.

III, 27

Prayer

Thanks to Thee ever, O gentle Christ,
    That Thou hast raised me freely from the black
And from the darkness of last night
    To the kindly light of this day.

Praise unto Thee, O God of all creatures,
    According to each life Thou hast poured on me,
My desire, my word, my sense, my repute,
My thought, my deed, my way, my fame.

III, 29

Morning Prayer

Thanks be to Thee, Jesus Christ,
Who brought'st me up from last night,
To the gladsome light of this day,
To win everlasting life for my soul,
Through the blood Thou didst shed for me.

Praise be to Thee, O God, for ever,
For the blessings Thou didst bestow on me—
My food, my speech, my work, my health,

. . . . .

And I beseech Thee
To shield me from sin,
To shield me from ill,
To sain* me this night,
And I low and poor,
O God of the poor!
O Christ of the wounds!
Give me wisdom along with Thy grace.

May the Holy One claim me,
And protect me on sea and on land,
And lead me on from step to step,
To the peace of the Everlasting City,
    The peace of the Everlasting City!

III, 97

*sain: to cross oneself or to make the sign of the cross
on a thing or person as a sign of consecration or blessing,
or to ward off evil influences

Supplication

O Being of life!
    O Being of peace!
    O Being of time!
        O Being of eternity!
        O Being of eternity!

Keep me in good means,
    Keep me in good intent,
Keep me in good estate,
    Better than I know to ask,
    Better than I know to ask!

Shepherd me this day,
    Relieve my distress,
Enfold me this night,
    Pour upon me Thy grace,
    Pour upon me Thy grace!

Guard for me my speech,
    Strengthen for me my love,
Illume for me the stream,
    Succor Thou me in death,
    Succor Thou me in death!

III, 55

The Dedication

Thanks to Thee, God,
Who brought'st me from yesterday
To the beginning of today,
Everlasting joy
To earn for my soul
With good intent.
And for every gift of peace
Thou bestowest on me,
My thoughts, my words,
My deeds, my desires
I dedicate to Thee.
I supplicate Thee,
I beseech Thee,
To keep me from offense,
And to shield me tonight,
For the sake of Thy wounds
With Thine offering of grace.

I, 99

Thanksgiving

Thanks to Thee, O God, that I have risen today,
To the rising of this life itself;
May it be to Thine own glory, O God of every gift,
And to the glory of my soul likewise.

O great God, aid Thou my soul
With the aiding of Thine own mercy;
Even as I clothe my body with wool,
Cover Thou my soul with the shadow of Thy wing.

Help me to avoid every sin,
　　And the source of every sin to forsake;
And as the mist scatters on the crest of the hills,
　　May each ill haze clear from my soul, O God.

III, 31

The Three

In name of Father,
In name of Son,
In name of Spirit,
　　Three in One:

Father cherish me,
Son cherish me,
Spirit cherish me,
　　Three all-kindly.

God make me holy,
Christ make me holy,
Spirit make me holy,
　　Three all-holy.

Three aid my hope,
Three aid my love,
Three aid mine eye,
　　And my knee from stumbling,
　　My knee from stumbling.

III, 63

God's Aid

God to enfold me,
    God to surround me,
God in my speaking,
    God in my thinking.

God in my sleeping,
    God in my waking,
God in my watching,
    God in my hoping.

God in my life,
    God in my lips,
God in my soul,
    God in my heart.

God in my sufficing,
    God in my slumber,
God in mine ever-living soul,
    God in mine eternity.

III, 53

The Guiding Light of Eternity

O God, who broughtest me from the rest of last night
Upon the joyous light of this day,
Be Thou bringing me from the new light of this day
Unto the guiding light of eternity.
    Oh! from the new light of this day
    Unto the guiding light of eternity.

I, 33

Farming
and Fishing

SONG AND RITUAL accompanied work on land and sea, many of the rituals picturesque and undoubtedly combining many residual pagan elements, always performed with much care and solemnity. The preparation of the seed-corn was of great importance.[1] Three days before it was sown a man would walk round it sunwise and sprinkle it with clear, cold water in the name of the Trinity. This moistening would hasten its growth. The actual sowing would begin on a Friday, a day which was held to be auspicious for all operations not necessitating the use of iron. The day of reaping was equally a day of ceremony, when the whole family would repair to the field dressed in their best and the father, taking up his sickle and facing the sun, would cut a handful of corn. Putting this sunwise round his head three times he began the reaping salutation which the others then took up, thanking the God of the harvest who gave them "corn and bread, food and flocks, wool and clothing, health and strength, and peace and plenty."[2]

Beltane, which was celebrated on May 1 each year, was a ritual to safeguard people and cattle from "murrain and mischance" for the coming year. All fires in the district were extinguished except for one lit on a knoll which was divided into two so that all, humans and animals, could rush through it for their purification and protection.[3]

Herding songs sung by whoever was driving the cows—men, women or children—commended the animals to the protection of the saints and asked for their safekeeping from all dangers and hazards of the terrain. The singer would use slow, measured cadences and often the measured tread of the older cattle would keep in time to the familiar music.[4]

Sea prayers and hymns were common. Before setting out, the voyagers stood round the boat and prayed to the God of the elements for a peaceful voyage over the stormy sea.[5] There were a number of fishing traditions, for example, that on Christmas day the young men went out to fish and the catch was distributed among the widows, orphans and poor. The 707 strokes refers to the saying among the people "that Christ required Peter to row that number of strokes straight out from the shore when He commanded him to go and procure the fish containing the tribute-money," and this was also required from the young men casting their lines on Christmas day.[6]

1. *pp. 24–5;* see I, 242—3.
2. I, 246–7.
3. *pp. 26–7;* see I, 182–3.
4. *pp. 27–31;* see I, 272–3 and IV, 40–1.
5. *pp. 33–4.*
6. *pp. 34–5;* see I, 318–19.

Reaping Blessing

God, bless Thou Thyself my reaping,
Each ridge, and plain, and field,
Each sickle curved, shapely, hard,
Each ear and handful in the sheaf,
    Each ear and handful in the sheaf.

Bless each maiden and youth,
Each woman and tender youngling,
Safeguard them beneath Thy shield of strength,
And guard them in the house of the saints,
    Guard them in the house of the saints.

Encompass each goat, sheep and lamb,
Each cow and horse, and store,
Surround Thou the flocks and herds,
And tend them to a kindly fold,
    Tend them to a kindly fold.

For the sake of Michael head of hosts,
Of Mary fair-skinned branch of grace,
Of Bride smooth-white of ringleted locks,
Of Columba of the graves and tombs,
    Columba of the graves and tombs.

I, 247

The Consecration of the Seed

I will go out to sow the seed,
In name of Him who gave it growth;
I will place my front in the wind,
And throw a gracious handful on high.
Should a grain fall on a bare rock,
It shall have no soil in which to grow;
As much as falls into the earth,
The dew will make it to be full.

Friday, day auspicious,
The dew will come down to welcome
Every seed that lay in sleep
Since the coming of cold without mercy;
Every seed will take root in the earth,
As the King of the elements desired,
The braird* will come forth with the dew,
It will inhale life from the soft wine.

I will come round with my step,
I will go rightways with the sun,
In name of Ariel and the angels nine,
In name of Gabriel and the Apostles kind.
Father, Son, and Spirit Holy,
Be giving growth and kindly substance
To every thing that is in my ground,
Till the day of gladness shall come.

The Feast day of Michael, day beneficent,
I will put my sickle round about
The root of my corn as was wont;
I will lift the first cut quickly;

I will put it three turns round
My head, saying my rune the while,
My back to the airt* of the north;
My face to the fair sun of power.

I, 243–5

* *braird:* the first shoots of corn or grass to sprout
* *airt: a* quarter of the compass

The Clipping Blessing

Go shorn and come woolly,
Bear the Beltane female lamb,
Be the lovely Bride thee endowing,
And the fair Mary thee sustaining,
    The fair Mary sustaining thee.

Michael the chief be shielding thee
From the evil dog and from the fox,
From the wolf and from the sly bear,
And from the taloned birds of destructive bills,
    From the taloned birds of hooked bills.

I, 293

The Beltane Blessing

Bless, O Threefold true and bountiful,
Myself, my spouse, and my children,
My tender children and their beloved mother at their head.
On the fragrant plain, on the gay mountain sheiling,
 On the fragrant plain, on the gay mountain sheiling.

Everything within my dwelling or in my possession,
All kine and crops, all flocks and corn,
From Hallow Eve to Beltane Eve,
With goodly progress and gentle blessing,
From sea to sea, and every river mouth,
 From wave to wave, arid base of waterfall.

Be the Three Persons taking possession of all to me
   belonging,
Be the sure Trinity protecting me in truth;
Oh! satisfy my soul in the words of Paul,
And shield my loved ones beneath the wing of Thy glory,
 Shield my loved ones beneath the wing of Thy glory.

Bless everything and every one,
Of this little household by my side;
Place the cross of Christ on us with the power of love,
Till we see the land of joy,
 Till we see the land of joy.

What time the kine shall forsake the stalls,
What time the sheep shall forsake the folds,
What time the goats shall ascend to the mount of mist,
May the tending of the Triune follow them,
 May the tending of the Triune follow them.

Thou Being who didst create me at the beginning,
Listen and attend me as I bend the knee to Thee,
Morning and evening as is becoming in me,
In Thine own presence, O God of life,
 In Thine own presence, O God of life.

 I, 183–5

Driving the Cows

Closed to you be every pit,
Smooth to you be every hill,
Snug to you be every bare spot,
 Beside the cold mountains.

The sanctuary of Mary Mother be yours,
The sanctuary of Brigit the loved be yours,
The sanctuary of Michael victorious be yours,
 Active and full be you gathered home.

The protection of shapely Cormac be yours,
The protection of Brendan of the ship be yours,
The protection of Maol Duinne the saint be yours
 In marshy ground and rocky ground.

The fellowship of Mary Mother be yours,
The fellowship of Brigit of kine be yours,
The fellowship of Michael victorious be yours,
 In nibbling, in chewing, in munching.

 IV, 41

Columba's Herding

May the herding of Columba
Encompass you going and returning,
Encompass you in strath* and on ridge
    And on the edge of each rough region;

May it keep you from pit and from mire,
Keep you from hill and from crag,
Keep you from loch and from downfall,
    Each evening and each darkling;

May it keep you from the mean destroyer,
Keep you from the mischievous niggard,
Keep you from the mishap of bar-stumbling
    And from the untoward fays.

The peace of Columba be yours in the grazing,
The peace of Brigit be yours in the grazing,
The peace of Mary be yours in the grazing,
    And may you return home safe-guarded.

    IV, 47

*strath: a wide valley, or low-lying land traversed by a river

Ho, My Heifer!

The night the Herdsman was out
No shackle went on a cow,
Lowing ceased not from the mouth of calf
Wailing the Herdsman of the flock,
    Wailing the Herdsman of the flock.

Ho my heifer! ho my heifer!
Ho my heifer! my heifer beloved!
My heartling heart, kind, fond,
For the sake of the High King take to thy calf.

The night the Herdsman was missing,
In the Temple He was found.
The King of the moon to come hither!
The King of the sun down from heaven!
King of the sun down from heaven!

I, 267

A Herding Croon

The cattle are today going a-flitting,
Hīll-i-rūin is o h-ūg o,
Ho ro la ill o,
Hīll-i-rūin is o h-ūg o,
Going to eat the grass of the burial-place,
Hīll-i-rūin is o h-ūg o,
Their own herdsman there to tend them,
Ho ro la ill o,
Hīll-i-rūin is o h-ūg o,
Tending them, fending them, turning them,
Hīll-i-rūin is o h-ūg o,
Be the gentle Bride milking them,
Hīll-i-rūin is o h-ūg o,
Be the lovely Mary keeping them,
Hīll-i-rūin is o h-ūg o,
And Jesu Christ at the end of their journey.
Hīll-i-rūin is o h-ūg o,

I, 283

The Protection of the Cattle

Pastures smooth, long, and spreading,
Grassy meads aneath your feet,
The friendship of God the Son to bring you home
To the field of the fountains,
    Field of the fountains.

Closed be every pit to you,
Smoothed be every knoll to you,
Cosy every exposure to you.
Beside the cold mountains,
    Beside the cold mountains.

The care of Peter and of Paul,
The care of James and of John,
The care of Bride fair and of Mary Virgin,
To meet you and to tend you,
    Oh! the care of all the band
    To protect you and to strengthen you.

I, 279

Herding Blessing

I will place this flock before me,
As was ordained of the King of the world,
Bride to keep them, to watch them, to tend them,
On ben, on glen, on plain,
    Bride to keep them, to watch them, to tend them,
    On ben, on glen, on plain.

Arise, thou Bride the gentle, the fair,
Take thou thy lint, thy comb, and thy hair,
Since thou to them madest the noble charm,
To keep them from straying, to save them from harm,
    Since thou to them madest the noble charm,
    To keep them from straying, to save them from harm.

From rocks, from drifts, from streams,
From crooked passes, from destructive pits,
From the straight arrows of the slender banshee,
From the heart of envy, from the eye of evil,
    From the straight arrows of the slender banshee,
    From the heart of envy, from the eye of evil.

Mary Mother, tend thou the offspring all,
Bridge of the fair palms, guard thou my flocks,
Kindly Columba, thou saint of many powers,
Encompass thou the breeding cows, bestow on me herds,
    Kindly Columba, thou saint of many powers,
    Encompass thou the breeding cows,
        bestow on me herds.

I, 275

Ocean Blessing

God the Father all-powerful, benign,
Jesu the Son of tears and of sorrow,
With thy co-assistance, O! Holy Spirit.

The Three-One, ever-living, ever-mighty, everlasting,
Who brought the Children of Israel through the Red Sea,
And Jonah to land from the belly of the great creature
    of the ocean,

Who brought Paul and his companions in the ship,
From the torment of the sea, from the dolor of the waves,
From the gale that was great, from the storm
    that was heavy.

When the storm poured on the Sea of Galilee,

  . . . . .

Sain* us and shield and sanctify us,
Be Thou, King of the elements, seated at our helm,
And lead us in peace to the end of our journey.

With winds mild, kindly, benign, pleasant,
Without swirl, without whirl, without eddy,
That would do no harmful deed to us.

We ask all things of Thee, O God,
According to Thine own will and word.

    I, 329

*Sain: save

Sea Prayer

HELMSMAN	Blest be the boat.
CREW	God the Father bless her.
HELMSMAN	Blest be the boat.
CREW	God the Son bless her.
HELMSMAN	Blest be the boat.
CREW	God the Spirit bless her.

ALL
God the Father,
God the Son,
God the Spirit,
Bless the boat.

HELMSMAN	What can befall you
	And God the Father with you?
CREW	No harm can befall us.
HELMSMAN	What can befall you
	And God the Son with you?
CREW	No harm can befall us.
HELMSMAN	What can befall you
	And God the Spirit with you?
CREW	No harm can befall us.

ALL
God the Father,
God the Son,
God the Spirit,
With us eternally.

HELMSMAN	What can cause you anxiety
	And the God of the elements over you?
CREW	No anxiety can be ours.

HELMSMAN	What can cause you anxiety And the King of the elements over you?
CREW	No anxiety can be ours.
ALL	The God of the elements, The King of the elements, The Spirit of the elements, Close over us, Ever eternally.

I, 333–5

Fishing Blessing

The day of light has come upon us,
Christ is born of the Virgin.

In His name I sprinkle the water
Upon every thing within my court.

Thou King of deeds and powers above,
Thy fishing blessing pour down on us.

I will sit me down with an oar in my grasp,
I will row me seven hundred and seven strokes.

I will cast down my hook,
The first fish which I bring up

In the name of Christ, King of the elements,
The poor shall have it at his wish.

And the king of fishers, the brave Peter,
He will after it give me his blessing.

Ariel, Gabriel, and John,
Raphael benign, and Paul,

Columba, tender in every distress,
And Mary fair, the endowed of grace.

Encompass ye us to the fishing-bank of ocean,
And still ye to us the crest of the waves.

Be the King of kings at the end of our course,
Of lengthened life and of lasting happiness.

Be the crown of the King from the Three on high,
Be the cross of Christ adown to shield us,
The crown of the King from the Three above,
The cross of Christ adown to shield us.

I, 319–21

Household Prayers

At the start of the day, as the housewife kindles the fire by lifting the peats so that the flame smothered (or smoored) the night before may spring again into life, she prays that the fire may be blessed to her and to the household and to the glory of God who gave it. Fire was never taken for granted but rather regarded as a miracle of divine power, provided not only to warm their bodies and cook their food but to remind them that they too, like fire, need constant renewal mentally and physically.[1] The ceremony of smooring the fire at night would also be performed symbolically and with loving care. The embers would be spread evenly on the hearth in the middle of the floor, and formed into a circle which would then be divided into three equal sections around a boss in the center. A peat was laid between each section, the first laid down in the name of the God of life, the second the God of peace, the third the God of grace. The circle would then be covered over with ashes sufficient to subdue but not extinguish the fire in the name of the three of light. When this was done the woman stretched out her hand and quietly intoned a smooring prayer.[2]

When she sat down to milk, the woman would sing and croon, secular songs and religious songs mixed and mingled, until each cow had been milked, her singing in unison with the movement of her hands. These milking croons[3] are especially varied and numerous, sung to pretty airs to please the cows and induce them to give their milk. Carmichael greatly enjoyed the sight of three or four girls with good voices among a fold of sixty, eighty, or a hundred picturesque Highland cows on a meadow or mountain slope. It encouraged some of his most colorful writing.

> The moaning and heaving of the sea afar, the swish of the wave on the shore, the caroling of the lark in the sky, the unbroken song of the mavis on the rock, the broken melody of the merle in the brake, the lowing of the kine without, the response of the calves within the fold, the singing of the milkmaids in unison with the movement of their hands, and of the soft sound of the snowy milk falling into the pail, the gilding of hill and dale, the glowing of the distant ocean beyond, as the sun sinks into the sea of golden glory, constitute a scene which the observer would not, if he could, forget.[4]

In winter in particular the women would be kept hard at work, early and late, at the whole process of making cloth. After it had been woven it would be "waulked," that is, stretched on a frame to strengthen and thicken it, a communal activity in which a number of women would range themselves round the trestles and sing as they worked. When this was done, one of them, the consecrator or celebrant, would place the roll of cloth in the center of the frame and name each member of the household for whom it was intended.

> This is not cloth for priest or cleric,
> But it is cloth for my own little Donald of love,
> For my companion beloved, for John of joy,
> And for Muriel of loveliest hue.

Then the cloth was spat upon and slowly reversed end by end in the name of the Trinity until it stood in the center of the frame.[5]

All work stopped on a Saturday night when every woman would tie up her loom and hang a crucifix above it to ward away all evil spirits.[6]

The quern blessing would be sung by women while grinding corn, as they filled it with one hand and turned it with the other, the songs composed in a meter to suit the rhythmic motion of the body at work.[7]

1. *pp. 38–9*; see I, 230–1.
2. *pp. 40–1;* see I, 234–5.
3. *pp. 41–4.*
4. See I, 258–9.
5. *pp. 47–8;* see I, 307.
6. *pp. 46–7.*
7. *pp. 48–9.*

Blessing of the Kindling

I will kindle my fire this morning
In presence of the holy angels of heaven,
In presence of Ariel of the loveliest form,
In presence of Uriel of the myriad charms,
Without malice, without jealousy, without envy,
Without fear, without terror of any one under the sun,
But the Holy Son of God to shield me.

    Without malice, without jealousy, without envy,
    Without fear, without terror of any one under the sun,
    But the Holy Son of God to shield me.

God, kindle Thou in my heart within
A flame of love to my neighbor,
To my foe, to my friend, to my kindred all,
To the brave, to the knave, to the thrall,
O Son of the loveliest Mary,
From the lowliest thing that liveth,
To the Name that is highest of all.
> O Son of the loveliest Mary,
> From the lowliest thing that liveth,
> To the Name that is highest of all.

I, 231

Kindling the Fire

I will raise the hearth-fire
As Mary would.
The encirclement of Bride and of Mary
On the fire, and on the floor,
And on the household all.

Who are they on the bare floor?
John and Peter and Paul.
Who are they by my bed?
The lovely Bride and her Fosterling.
Who are those watching over my sleep?
The fair loving Mary and her Lamb.
Who is that anear me?
The King of the sun, He himself it is.
Who is that at the back of my head?
The Son of Life without beginning, without time.

I, 233

Smooring the Fire

The sacred Three
To save,
To shield,
To surround
The hearth,
The house,
The household,
This eve,
This night,
Oh! this eve,
This night,
And every night,
Each single night.
        Amen.

I, 235

Smooring the Fire

I will build the hearth,
As Mary would build it.
The encompassment of Bride and of Mary,
Guarding the hearth, guarding the floor,
Guarding the household all.

Who are they on the lawn without?
Michael the sun-radiant of my trust.
Who are they on the middle of the floor?
John and Peter and Paul.
Who are they by the front of my bed?
Sun-bright Mary and her Son.

The mouth of God ordained,
The angel of God proclaimed,
An angel white in charge of the hearth
Till white day shall come to the embers.
An angel white in charge of the hearth
Till white day shall come to the embers.

I, 237

Prayer of the Teats

Teat of Mary,
Teat of Brigit,
Teat of Michael,
    Teat of God.

No malice shall lie,
No envy shall lie,
No eye shall lie
    Upon my heart's dear one.

No fear shall lie,
No ill—will shall lie,
No loss shall lie
    On my own "Mineag."*

No spell shall lie,
No spite shall lie
On her beneath the keeping
    Of the King of the stars;
On her beneath the keeping
    Of the King of the stars.

IV, 63

*Mineag: a soft, gentle girl or woman

Give the Milk, My Treasure

Give the milk, my treasure!
Give the milk, my treasure!
Give the milk, my treasure!

> Give the milk
> And thou'lt get a reward,—
> Bannock of quern,
> Sap of ale-wort,
> Wine of chalice,
> Honey and the wealth of the milk,
> > My treasure!

> Give the milk
> And thou'lt get a reward,—
> Grasses of the plain,
> Milk of the fields,
> Ale of the malt,
> Music of the lyre,
> > My treasure!

Give the milk, my treasure!
Give the milk, my treasure!

> Give the milk
> And thou'lt have the blessing
> Of the King of the earth,
> The King of the sea,
> The King of heaven,
> The King of the angels,
> The King of the City,
> > My treasure!

Give the milk, my treasure,
Give quietly, with steady flow,
Give the milk, my treasure,
    With steady flow and calmly.

IV, 65–7

Milking Croon

Come, Brendan, from the ocean,
Come, Ternan, most potent of men,
Come, Michael valiant, down
And propitiate to me the cow of my joy.
    Ho my heifer, ho heifer of my love,
    Ho my heifer, ho heifer of my love.
    My beloved heifer, choice cow of every shieling,
    For the sake of the High King take to thy calf.

Come, beloved Colum of the fold,
Come, great Bride of the flocks,
Come, fair Mary from the cloud,
And propitiate to me the cow of my love.
    Ho my heifer, ho heifer of my love.

The stock-dove will come from the wood,
The tusk will come from the wave,
The fox will come but not with wiles,
To hail my cow of virtues.
    Ho my heifer, ho heifer of my love.

I, 259

Milking Song

Come, Mary, and milk my cow,
Come, Bride, and encompass her,
Come, Columba the benign
    And twine thine arms around my cow.
        Ho my heifer, ho my gentle heifer,
        Ho my heifer, ho my gentle heifer,
        Ho my heifer, ho my gentle heifer,
        My heifer dear, generous and kind,
            For the sake of the High King take to thy calf.

Come, Mary Virgin, to my cow,
Come, great Bride, the beauteous,
Come, thou milkmaid of Jesus Christ,
    And place thine arms beneath my cow.
        Ho my heifer, ho my gentle heifer.

Lovely black cow, pride of the shieling,
First cow of the byre, choice mother of calves,
Wisps of straw round the cows of the townland,
    A shackle of silk on my heifer beloved.
        Ho my heifer, ho my gentle heifer.

My black cow, my black cow
A like sorrow afflicts me and thee,
Thou grieving for thy lovely calf,
    I for my beloved son under the sea,
        My beloved only son under the sea.

I, 271

Invocation at Churning

Come, thou Calum Cille* kindly,
    Hasten the luster on the cream;
Seest thou the orphans unregarded
    Waiting the blessing of the milk-wave of the kine.

      Stillim! steòilim!
      Strichim! streòichim!
      Send down the broken
    And bring up the whole!

Come, thou Brigit, handmaid calm,
    Hasten the butter on the cream;
Seest thou impatient Peter yonder
    Waiting the buttered bannock white and yellow.

      Stillim! steòilim!
      Strichim! streòichim!
      Send down the broken
    And bring up the whole!

Come, thou Mary Mother mild,
    Hasten the butter on the cream;
Seest thou Paul and John and Jesus
    Waiting the gracious butter yonder.

      Stillim! steòilim!
      Strichim! streòichim!
      Send down the broken
    And bring up the whole!

IV, 87

Calum Cille: the Irish form of Columba

Milking Prayer

Bless, O God, my little cow,
    Bless, O God, my desire;
Bless Thou my partnership
    And the milking of my hands, O God.

Bless, O God, each teat,
    Bless, O God, each finger;
Bless Thou each drop
    That goes into my pitcher, O God!

IV, 65

Loom Blessing

Bless, O Chief of generous chiefs,
My loom and everything a-near me,
Bless me in my every action,
Make Thou me safe while I live.

From every brownie and fairy woman,
From every evil wish and sorrow,
Help me, O Thou helping Being,
As long as I shall be in the land of the living.

In name of Mary, mild of deeds,
In name of Columba, just and potent,
Consecrate the four posts of my loom,
Till I begin on Monday.

Her pedals, her sleay,* and her shuttle,
Her reeds, her warp, and her cogs,
Her cloth-beam, and her thread-beam,
Thrums and the thread of the plies.

Every web, black, white, and fair,
Roan, dun, checked, and red,
Give Thy blessing everywhere,
On every shuttle passing under the thread.

Thus will my loom be unharmed,
Till I shall arise on Monday;
Beauteous Mary will give me of her love,
And there shall be no obstruction I shall not overcome.

I, 305

sleay: an instrument used in weaving to beat up the weft, that is, threads
that cross from side to side of a web at right angles to the warp

Chant of the Warping

My warp shall be very even,
Give to me Thy blessing, O God,
And to all who are beneath my roof
    In the dwelling.

Michael, thou angel of power,
Mary fair, who art above,
Christ, Thou Shepherd of the people,
Do ye your eternal blessing
    Bestow

On each one who shall lie down,
In name of the Father and of Christ,
And of the Spirit of peacefulness,
    And of grace.

Sprinkle down on us like dew
The gracious wisdom of the mild woman.
Who neglected never the guidance
    Of the High King.

Ward away every evil eye,
And all people of evil wishes,
Consecrate the woof and the warp
    Of every thread.

Place Thou Thine arm around
Each woman who shall be waulking it,
And do Thou aid her in the hour
    Of her need.

Give to me virtues abundant,
As Mary had in her day,
That I may possess the glory
    Of the High King.

I, 297

The Quern Blessing

On Ash Eve
We shall have flesh,
We should have that.
We should have that.

The cheek of hen,
Two bits of barley,
That were enough.
That were enough.

We shall have mead,
We shall have spruce,
We shall have wine,
We shall have feast.
We shall have sweetness and milk produce,
Honey and milk,
Wholesome ambrosia,
Abundance of that,
Abundance of that.

We shall have harp,
We shall have harp,
We shall have lute,
We shall have horn.
We shall have sweet psaltery
Of the melodious strings
And the regal lyre,
Of the songs we shall have,
Of the songs we shall have.

The calm fair Bride will be with us,
The gentle Mary mother will be with us.
Michael the chief
Of glancing glaves,*
And the King of kings
And Jesus Christ,
And the Spirit of peace
And of grace will be with us,
Of grace will be with us.

I, 255–7

*glaves: swords or lances

Night Prayers

MARY MACRAE, who gave the prayer that opens this section to Alexander Carmichael, told him, "After I have closed my door and put out my cruisie (lamp) and gone to my bed, I beseech the Being of life and the God of grace, and say to Him—O God of life, darken not to me Thy light."[1] Another old man, whom Carmichael described as "poor, aged and lonely," expanded on this night ritual.

> I do now as my mother was doing when I was a child. Before going to my bed I place the bar upon the leaf of the door, and I make the cross of Christ on the bar and on the door, and I supplicate the great God of life, the Father of all living, to protect and comfort me this night....After that I put out my light, and then I go to bed, and when I lie down on my pillow I make the cross of Christ upon my breast, over the tablet of my hard heart, and I beseech the living God of the universe—
>
> > May the Light of lights come
> > > To my dark heart from Thy place;
> > May the Spirit's wisdom come
> > > To my heart's tablet from my Savior.[2]

1. *p. 51;* see III, 343.
2. III, 337.

Repose of Sleep

O God of life, darken not to me Thy light,
O God of life, close not to me Thy joy,
O God of life, shut not to me Thy door,
    O God of life, refuse not to me Thy mercy,
    O God of life, quench Thou to me Thy wrath,
    And O God of life, crown Thou to me Thy gladness,
O God of life, crown Thou to me Thy gladness.

III, 343

The Sleep Prayer

I am now going into the sleep,
Be it that I in health shall waken;
If death be to me in the death-sleep,
Be it that on Thine own arm,
O God of Grace, I in peace shall waken;
    Be it on Thine own beloved arm,
    O God of Grace, that I in peace shall waken.

Be my soul on Thy right hand, O God,
Thou King of the heaven of heavens;
Thou it was who bought'st me with Thy blood,
Thou it was who gavest Thy life for me,
    Encompass Thou me this night, O God,
    That no harm, no evil shall me befall.

Whilst the body is dwelling in the sleep,
The soul is soaring in the shadow of heaven,
Be the red-white Michael meeting the soul,
Early and late, night and day,
    Early and late, night and day. Amen.

I, 85

Sleeping Prayer

I am placing my soul and my body
On Thy sanctuary this night, O God,
On Thy sanctuary, O Jesus Christ,
On Thy sanctuary, O Spirit of perfect truth,
 The Three who would defend my cause,
 Nor turn Their backs upon me.

Thou, Father, who art kind and just,
Thou, Son, who didst overcome death,
Thou, Holy Spirit of power,
Be keeping me this night from harm;
 The Three who would justify me
 Keeping me this night and always.

 I, 73

Going to Rest

May the Light of lights come
 To my dark heart from Thy place;
May the Spirit's wisdom come
 To my heart's tablet from my Savior.

 Be the peace of the Spirit mine this night,
 Be the peace of the Son mine this night,
 Be the peace of the Father mine this night,
 The peace of all peace be mine this night,
Each morning and evening of my life.

 III, 337

I Lie in My Bed

I lie in my bed
As I would lie in the grave,
Thine arm beneath my neck,
    Thou Son of Mary victorious.

Angels shall watch me
And I lying in slumber,
And angels shall guard me
    In the sleep of the grave.

Uriel shall be at my feet,
Ariel shall be at my back,
Gabriel shall be at my head,
    And Raphael shall be at my side.

Michael shall be with my soul,
The strong shield of my love!
And the Physician Son of Mary
Shall put the salve to mine eye,
    The Physician Son of Mary
    Shall put the salve to mine eye!

I, 95

Bed Blessing

I am lying down tonight as beseems
In the fellowship of Christ, son of the Virgin of ringlets.
In the fellowship of the gracious Father of glory,
In the fellowship of the Spirit of powerful aid.

I am lying down tonight with God,
And God tonight will lie down with me,
I will not lie down tonight with sin, nor shall
Sin nor sin's shadow lie down with me.

I am lying down tonight with the Holy Spirit,
And the Holy Spirit this night will lie down with me,
I will lie down this night with the Three of my love,
And the Three of my love will lie down with me.

I, 83

Sleep Consecration

I lie down tonight
With fair Mary and with her Son,
With pure-white Michael,
And with Bride beneath her mantle.

I lie down with God,
And God will lie down with me,
I will not lie down with Satan,
Nor shall Satan lie down with me.

O God of the poor,
Help me this night,
Omit me not entirely
From Thy treasure-house.

For the many wounds
That I inflicted on Thee,
I cannot this night
Enumerate them.

Thou King of the blood of truth,
Do not forget me in Thy dwelling-place,
Do not exact from me for my transgressions,
Do not omit me in Thine ingathering.
    In Thine ingathering.

I, 81

Night Prayer

In Thy name, O Jesu Who wast crucified,
    I lie down to rest;
Watch Thou me in sleep remote,
    Hold Thou me in Thy one hand;
        Watch Thou me in sleep remote,
            Hold Thou me in Thy one hand.

Bless me, O my Christ,
    Be Thou my shield protecting me,
Aid my steps in the pitful swamp,
    Lead Thou me to the life eternal;
        Aid my steps in the pitful swamp,
            Lead Thou me to the life eternal.

Keep Thou me in the presence of God,
    O good and gracious Son of the Virgin,
And fervently I pray Thy strong protection
    From my lying down at dusk to my rising at day;
        And fervently I pray Thy strong protection
            From my lying down at dusk to my rising
            at day.

III, 329–31

Sleep Prayer

O Jesu without sin,
King of the poor,
Who wert sorely subdued
Under ban of the wicked,
Shield Thou me this night
    From Judas.

My soul on Thine own arm, O Christ,
Thou the King of the City of Heaven,
Thou it was who bought'st my soul, O Jesu,
    Thou it was who didst sacrifice Thy life for me.

Protect Thou me because of my sorrow,
For the sake of Thy passion, Thy wounds,
        and Thine own blood,
And take me in safety tonight
    Near to the City of God.

I, 77

Resting Blessing

In name of the Lord Jesus,
And of the Spirit of healing balm,
In name of the Father of Israel,
    I lay me down to rest.

If there be evil threat or quirk,
Or covert act intent on me,
God free me and encompass me,
    And drive from me mine enemy.

In name of the Father precious,
And of the Spirit of healing balm,
In name of the Lord Jesus,
    I lay me down to rest.

. . . . .

        God, help me and encompass me,
    From this hour till the hour of my death.

I, 79

I Lie Down This Night

I lie down this night with God,
    And God will lie down with me;
I lie down this night with Christ,
    And Christ will lie down with me;
I lie down this night with Spirit,
    And the Spirit will lie down with me;
God and Christ and the Spirit
    Be lying down with me.

III, 333

Thou Great God

Thou great God, grant me Thy light,
    Thou great God, grant me Thy grace,
Thou great God, grant me Thy joy,
    And let me be made pure in the well of Thy health.

Lift Thou from me, O God, my anguish,
    Lift Thou from me, O God, my abhorrence,
Lift Thou from me, O God, all empty pride,
    And lighten my soul in the light of Thy love.

As I put off from me my raiment,
    Grant me to put off my struggling;
As the haze rises from off the crest of the mountains,
    Raise Thou my soul from the vapor of death.

Jesu Christ, O Son of Mary,
    Jesu Christ, O Paschal Son,
Shield my body in the shielding of Thy mantle,
    And make pure my soul in the purifying of Thy grace.

III, 345

The Soul Plaint

O Jesu! tonight,
Thou Shepherd of the poor,
Thou sinless person
Who didst suffer full sore,
By ban of the wicked,
And wast crucified.

Save me from evil,
Save me from harm,
Save Thou my body,
Sanctify me tonight,
O Jesu! tonight,
Nor leave me.

Endow me with strength,
Thou Herdsman of might,
Guide me aright,
Guide me in Thy strength,
O Jesu! in Thy strength
Preserve me.

I, 71

The Pilgrims' Safeguarding

I am placing my soul and my body
Under thy guarding this night, O Brigit,
O calm Fostermother of the Christ without sin,
O calm Fostermother of the Christ of wounds.

I am placing my soul and my body
Under thy guarding this night, O Mary,
O tender Mother of the Christ of the poor,
O tender Mother of the Christ of tears.

I am placing my soul and my body
Under Thy guarding this night, O Christ,
O Thou Son of the tears, of the wounds, of the piercings,
May Thy cross this night be shielding me.

I am placing my soul and my body
Under Thy guarding this night, O God,
O Thou Father of help to the poor feeble pilgrims,
Protector of earth and of heaven,
    Protector of earth and of heaven.

III, 321

Birth and Death

BIRTH AND DEATH, the two great events of life, had many ceremonies attached to them. After the birth the child would be handed across the fire three times, and then carried sunwise three times round the fire, no doubt reflecting some pre-Christian ritual. But then the midwife continued with a further ritual which is best captured in her own words to Carmichael.

> When the image of the God of life is born into the world I put three little drops of water on the child's forehead. I put the first little drop in the name of the Father, and the watching-women say Amen. I put the second little drop in the name of the Son, and the watching-women say Amen. I put the third little drop in the name of the Spirit, and the watching-women say Amen. And I beseech the Holy Three to lave and to bathe the child and to preserve it to Themselves. And the watching-women say Amen. All the people in the house are raising their voices with the watching-women, giving witness that the child has been committed to the blessed Trinity. By the Book itself! ear has never heard music more beautiful than the music of the watching-women when they are consecrating the seed of man and committing him to the great God of life.

Eight days later the child would be baptized and received formally into the Church; "great baptism" or "clerical baptism" in distinction to the first "birth baptism."[1]

Death blessings were also known as "soul leading" or "soul peace." A soul-friend, the "anam-chara," almost always a layperson, would sing or intone the soul peace over the dying person, and all present would join in beseeching the three persons of the Godhead and all the saints of Heaven to receive the departing soul. During the prayer the soul-friend would make the sign of the cross with the right thumb over the lips of the dying. It was an occasion which drew from Alexander Carmichael some of his more colorful prose.

> The scene is touching and striking in the extreme, and the man or woman is not to be envied who could witness unmoved the distress of these lovable people of the West taking leave of those who are near and dear to them in their pilgrimage, as they say, of crossing the black river of death; the great ocean of darkness; and the mountains of eternity. The scene may be in a lowly cot begrimed with smoke and black with age, but the heart is not less warm, the tear not less bitter, and the parting not less distressful, than in the court of the noble or in the palace of royalty.[2]

He was also moved by an account of a funeral at which "I am going home with thee" was sung—characteristically to the air of a secular song. He spoke to people who had heard it in Lewis.

> They said that the scene and the tune were singularly impressive—the moaning of the sea, the mourning of the women, and the lament of the pipes over all as the body was carried to its home of winter, to its home of autumn, of spring and of summer; never could they forget the solemnity of the occasion, where all was so natural and so beautiful, and nature seemed to join in the feelings of humanity.[3]

1. *pp. 63–5;* see III, 3.
2. I, 116–17.
3. *p. 73;* see III, 379.

Birth Baptism

In name of Father,

    Amen.

In name of Son,

    Amen.

In name of Spirit,

    Amen.

Three to lave thee,

    Amen.

Three to bathe thee,

    Amen.

Three to save thee,

    Amen.

Father and Son and Spirit,

    Amen.

Father and Son and Spirit,

    Amen.

Father and Son and Spirit,

    Amen.

III, 11

A Small Drop of Water

A small drop of water
    To thy forehead, beloved,
Meet for Father, Son and Spirit,
    The Triune of power.

A small drop of water
    To encompass my beloved,
Meet for Father, Son and Spirit,
    The Triune of power.

A small drop of water
    To fill thee with each grace,
Meet for Father, Son and Spirit,
    The Triune of power.

III, 21–3

The Baptism by the Knee-Woman

In name of God,
In name of Jesus,
In name of Spirit,
The perfect Three of power.

The little drop of the Father
On thy little forehead, beloved one.

The little drop of the Son
On thy little forehead, beloved one.

The little drop of the Spirit
On thy little forehead, beloved one.

To aid thee, to guard thee,
To shield thee, to surround thee.

To keep thee from the fays,
To shield thee from the host.

To save thee from the gnome,
To deliver thee from the specter.

The little drop of the Three
To shield thee from the sorrow.

The little drop of the Three
To fill thee with Their pleasantness.

The little drop of the Three
To fill thee with Their virtue.

O the little drop of the Three
To fill thee with Their virtue.

III, 17–19

The Soul Leading

Be this soul on Thine arm, O Christ,
Thou King of the City of Heaven. Amen.

Since Thou, O Christ, it was who bought'st this soul,
Be its peace on Thine own keeping. Amen.

And may the strong Michael, high king of the angels,
Be preparing the path before this soul, O God. Amen.

Oh! the strong Michael in peace with thee, soul,
And preparing for thee the way to the kingdom of the
      Son of God. Amen.

   I, 117

Soul Peace

Since Thou Christ it was who didst buy the soul—
At the time of yielding the life,
At the time of pouring the sweat,
At the time of offering the clay,
At the time of shedding the blood,
At the time of balancing the beam,
At the time of severing the breath,
At the time of delivering the judgment,
Be its peace upon Thine own ingathering,
Jesus Christ Son of gentle Mary,
Be its peace upon Thine own ingathering,
     O Jesus! upon Thine own ingathering.

And may Michael white kindly,
High king of the holy angels,
Take possession of the beloved soul,
And shield it home to the Three of surpassing love,
    Oh! to the Three of surpassing love.

    I, 121

Death Prayer

O God, give me of Thy wisdom
O God, give me of Thy mercy,
O God, give me of Thy fullness,
    And of Thy guidance in face of every strait.

O God, give me of Thy holiness,
O God, give me of Thy shielding,
O God, give me of Thy surrounding,
    And of Thy peace in the knot of my death.

Oh give me of Thy surrounding,
    And of Thy peace at the hour of my death!

    III, 375

The Death Dirge

Thou goest home this night to thy home of winter,
To thy home of autumn, of spring, and of summer;
Thou goest home this night to thy perpetual home,
To thine eternal bed, to thine eternal slumber.

> Sleep thou, sleep, and away with thy sorrow,
> Sleep thou, sleep, and away with thy sorrow,
> Sleep thou, sleep, and away with thy sorrow;
> Sleep, thou beloved, in the Rock of the fold.

Sleep this night in the breast of thy Mother,
Sleep, thou beloved, while she herself soothes thee;
Sleep thou this night on the Virgin's arm,
Sleep, thou beloved, while she herself kisses thee.

The great sleep of Jesus, the surpassing sleep of Jesus,
The sleep of Jesus' wound, the sleep of Jesus' grief,
The young sleep of Jesus, the restoring sleep of Jesus,
> The sleep of the kiss of Jesus of peace and of glory.

The sleep of the seven lights be thine, beloved,
The sleep of the seven joys be thine, beloved,
The sleep of the seven slumbers be thine, beloved,
On the arm of the Jesus of blessings, the Christ of grace.

> The shade of death lies upon thy face, beloved,
> But the Jesus of grace has His hand round about thee;
> > In nearness to the Trinity farewell to thy pains,
> Christ stands before thee and peace is in His mind.

Sleep, O sleep in the calm of all calm,
Sleep, O sleep in the guidance of guidance,
Sleep, O sleep in the love of all loves;
    Sleep, O beloved, in the Lord of life,
    Sleep, O beloved, in the God of life!

III, 383–5

The Death Blessing

God, omit not this woman from Thy covenant,
And the many evils which she in the body committed,
That she cannot this night enumerate.
    The many evils that she in the body committed,
    That she cannot this night enumerate.

Be this soul on Thine own arm, O Christ,
Thou King of the City of Heaven,
And since Thine it was, O Christ, to buy the soul,
At the time of the balancing of the beam,
At the time of the bringing in the judgment,
Be it now on Thine own right hand,
    Oh! on Thine own right hand.

And be the holy Michael, king of angels,
Coming to meet the soul,
And leading it home
To the heaven of the Son of God.
    The Holy Michael, high king of angels,
    Coming to meet the soul,
    And leading it home
    To the heaven of the Son of God.

I, 119

Joyous Death

Give Thou to me, O God,
    Each food that is needful for my body;
Give Thou to me, O God,
    Each light that is needful for my mind;
Give Thou to me, O God,
    Each salve that is needful for my soul.

Give Thou to me, O God,
    Sincere repentance;
Give Thou to me, O God,
    Whole-hearted repentance;
Give Thou to me, O God,
    Lasting repentance.

Give Thou to me, O God,
    The death of the priceless oil;
Give Thou to me, O God,
    That the Healer of my soul be near me;
Give Thou to me, O God,
    The death of joy and of peace.

Give Thou to me, O God,
    To confess the death of Christ;
Give Thou to me, O God,
    To meditate the agony of Christ;
Give Thou to me, O God,
    To make warm the love of Christ.

O great God of Heaven,
　　Draw Thou my soul to Thyself,
That I may make repentance
　　With a right and a strong heart,
With a heart broken and contrite,
　　That shall not change nor bend nor yield.

O great God of the angels,
　　Bring Thou me to the dwelling of peace;
O great God of the angels,
　　Preserve me from the evil of the fairies;
O great God of the angels,
　　Bathe me in the bathing of Thy pool.

O great God of grace,
　　Give Thou to me the strong Spirit of powers;
O great God of grace,
　　Give Thou to me the Spirit undying, everlasting;
O great God of grace,
　　Give Thou to me the loving Spirit of the Lamb.

III, 389–91

The Battle to Come

Jesus, Thou Son of Mary, I call on Thy name,
And on the name of John the apostle beloved,
And on the names of all the saints in the red domain,*
To shield me in the battle to come,
> To shield me in the battle to come.

When the mouth shall be closed,
When the eye shall be shut,
When the breath shall cease to rattle,
When the heart shall cease to throb,
> When the heart shall cease to throb.

When the Judge shall take the throne,
And when the cause is fully pleaded,
O Jesu, Son of Mary, shield Thou my soul,
O Michael fair, acknowledge my departure.
> O Jesu, Son of Mary, shield Thou my soul!
> O Michael fair, receive my departure!

III, 113

*saints in the red domain: probably a reference to the three types
of martyrdom in the Celtic church, the red being death
by the spilling of blood

I Am Going Home With Thee

I am going home with thee
    To thy home! to thy home!
I am going home with thee
    To thy home of winter.

I am going home with thee
    To thy home! to thy home!
I am going home with thee
    To thy home of autumn,
        of spring and of summer.

I am going home with thee,
    Thou child of my love,
To thine eternal bed,
    To thy perpetual sleep.

I am going home with thee,
    Thou child of my love,
To the dear Son of blessings,
    To the Father of grace.

III, 379–81

The Hearth

A SENSE OF KINSHIP unites those gathered around the hearth. Blessings upon the roof that shelters them, and upon the food that they share, come into this section.[1] But sons and daughters may have to leave the hearth to find work far away. The neighbors would come to say farewell, bringing bonnets, stockings, gloves and plaiding, gifts that they had made and which they offered with tears in their eyes and prayers in their hearts. This would be the setting for the mother's blessing.[2] Alexander Carmichael attended a number of these parting scenes and found them striking and impressive. An aged woman in Uist said "By the Book, love, you would not seek but listen to them although your own heart were full and overflowing and you striving to keep down the tears. O thou Mary of grace! O thou Mother of sore sorrow! Many the tearful eye that I have seen in my day and in my generation."[3]

1. *pp. 75–9.*
2. *pp. 81–4.*
3. III, 246–7.

Bless, O God, the Hearth

Bless, O God, the fire,
    As Thou didst bless the Virgin;
Bless, O God, the hearth,
    As Thou didst bless the Sabbath.
Bless, O God, the household,
    According as Jesus said;
Bless, O God, the family,
    As becomes us to offer it.
Bless, O God, the house,
    Bless, O God, the fire,
Bless, O God, the hearth;
    Be Thyself our stay.
        May the Being of life bless,
        May the Christ of love bless,
        May the Spirit Holy bless
    Each one and all,
    Every one and all.

III, 355

Blessing of House

God bless the house,
From site to stay,
From beam to wall,
From end to end,
From ridge to basement,
From balk to roof-tree,
From found to summit,
    Found and summit.

I, 105

Blessing of a House

Be Christ's cross on your new dwelling,
    Be Christ's cross on your new hearth,
Be Christ's cross on your new abode,
    Upon your new fire blazing.

Be Christ's cross on your topmost grain,
    Be Christ's cross on your fruitful wives,
Be Christ's cross on your virile sons,
    Upon your conceptive daughters.

Be Christ's cross on your serving-maid,
    Be Christ's cross on your knee of promise,
Be Christ's cross on your coming generation,
    Upon your prospering cattle.

Be Christ's cross on your means and portion,
    Be Christ's cross on your kin and people,
Be Christ's cross on you each light and darkness,
    Each day and each night of your lives,
    Each day and each night of your lives.

III, 367

House Protecting

God, bless the world and all that is therein.
God, bless my spouse and my children,
God, bless the eye that is in my head,
And bless, O God, the handling of my hand;
What time I rise in the morning early,
What time I lie down late in bed,
> Bless my rising in the morning early,
> And my lying down late in bed.

God, protect the house, and the household,
God, consecrate the children of the motherhood,
God, encompass the flocks and the young;
Be Thou after them and tending them,
What time the flocks ascend hill and wold,
What time I lie down to sleep,
> What time the flocks ascend hill and wold,
> What time I lie down in peace to sleep.

I,103

Peace

The peace of God, the peace of men,
The peace of Columba kindly,
The peace of Mary mild, the loving,
The peace of Christ, King of tenderness,
    The peace of Christ, King of tenderness,

Be upon each window, upon each door,
Upon each hole that lets in light,
Upon the four corners of my house,
Upon the four corners of my bed,
    Upon the four corners of my bed;

Upon each thing my eye takes in,
Upon each thing my mouth takes in,
Upon my body that is of earth
And upon my soul that came from on high,
    Upon my body that is of earth
    And upon my soul that came from on high.

III, 265

Peace

Peace between neighbors,
Peace between kindred,
Peace between lovers,
    In love of the King of life.

Peace between person and person,
Peace between wife and husband,
Peace between woman and children,
The peace of Christ above all peace.

Bless, O Christ, my face,
　　Let my face bless every thing;
Bless, O Christ, mine eye,
　　Let mine eye bless all it sees.

III, 267

Thanks for Food

Give us, O God, of the morning meal,
　　Benefit to the body, the frame of the soul;
Give us, O God, of the seventh bread,
　　Enough for our need at evening close.

Give us, O God, of the honey-sweet foaming milk,
　　The sap and milk of the fragrant farms,
And give us, O God, along with Thy sleep,
　　Rest in the shade of Thy covenant Rock.

Give us this night of the corn that shall last,
　　Give us this night of the drink that shall hurt not;
Give us this night, anear to the heavens,
　　The chalice of Mary mild, the tender.

Be with us by day, be with us by night,
　　Be with us by light and by dark,
In our lying down and in our rising up,
　　In speech, in walk, in prayer.

III, 313

Grace Before Food

Be with me, O God, at breaking of bread,
    Be with me, O God, at the close of my meal;
Let no whit adown my body
    That may hurt my sorrowing soul.
        O no whit adown my body
            That may hurt my sorrowing soul.

III, 315

Thanks After Food

Thanks be to Thee, O God,
Praise be to Thee, O God,
Reverence be to Thee, O God,
    For all Thou hast given me.

As Thou has given life corporeal
    To earn me my worldly food,
So grant me life eternal
    To show forth Thy glory.

Grant me grace throughout my life,
    Grant me life at the hour of my death;
Be with me, O God, in casting off my breath,
    O God, be with me in the deep currents.

O! in the parting of the breath,
    O! be with my soul in the deep currents.
O God, be with my soul in sounding the fords,
    In crossing the deep floods.

III, 317

Mother's Consecration

Be the great God between thy two shoulders,
To protect thee in thy going and in thy coming,
Be the Son of Mary Virgin near thine heart,
And be the perfect Spirit upon thee pouring—
Oh, the perfect Spirit upon thee pouring!

II, 171

The Mother's Blessing

The joy of God be in thy face,
    Joy to all who see thee,
The circle of God around thy neck,
    Angels of God shielding thee,
    Angels of God shielding thee.

Joy of night and day be thine,
Joy of sun and moon be thine,
Joy of men and women be thine,
    Each land and sea thou goest,
    Each land and see thou goest.

Be every season happy for thee,
Be every season bright for thee,
Be every season glad for thee,
    And the Son of Mary Virgin at peace with thee,
    The Son of Mary Virgin at peace with thee.

Be thine the compassing of the God of life,
Be thine the compassing of the Christ of love,
Be thine the compassing of the Spirit of Grace,
    To befriend thee and to aid thee,
        Donald,
    Thou beloved one of my breast.

(Oh! to befriend thee and to aid thee,
        Mary,
    Thou beloved one of my heart.)

III, 255

The Mother's Parting Blessing

The benison of God be to thee,
The benison of Christ be to thee,
The benison of Spirit be to thee,
And to thy children,
 To thee and to thy children.

The peace of God be to thee,
The peace of Christ be to thee,
The peace of Spirit be to thee,
During all thy life,
 All the days of thy life.

The keeping of God upon thee in every pass,
The shielding of Christ upon thee in every path,
The bathing of Spirit upon thee in every stream,
 In every land and sea thou goest.

The keeping of the everlasting Father be thine
 Upon His own illumined altar;
The keeping of the everlasting Father be thine
 Upon His own illumined altar.

III, 247

The Mother's Blessing

Where thou shalt bring the crown of thy head,
    Where thou shalt bring the tablet of thy brow,
Strength be to thee therein,
    Blest be to thee the powers therein;
        Strength be to thee therein,
            Blest be to thee the powers therein.

Lasting be thou in thy lying down,
    Lasting be thou in thy rising up,
Lasting be thou by night and by day,
    And surpassing good be heaven to my dear one;
        Lasting be thou by night and by day,
            And surpassing good be heaven to my dear one.

The face of God be to thy countenance,
The face of Christ the kindly,
The face of the Spirit Holy
    Be saving thee each hour
    In danger and in sorrow;
        Be saving thee each hour
        In danger and in sorrow.

III, 253

Journeys

ONE RECITER, Dugall MacAulay, a cottar of Benbecula, who gave Alexander Carmichael the journey prayer which appears on page 89, told him that he always recited this to himself, under his breath, whenever he went upon a journey, "however short the distance, however small the matter of his errand."[1] Such prayers are very much part of the Celtic tradition of commending the whole person and every activity to God and for asking protection. When anyone set out on a really long journey family and friends would join the traveler in singing the prayer for traveling and in starting the journey with them.[2]

Journey Blessings and the final prayer[3] are charms, worn on the person to safeguard the wearer against drowning at sea, against disaster on land, against evil eye, against being lifted by the hosts of the air, against being waylaid by fairies. The charm would consist of a word, a phrase, a saying or a verse from one of the Gospels. The words were written on paper or parchment, often illuminated and ornamented in Celtic design, and the script was placed in a small bag of linen and sewn into the waistcoat of a man and the bodice of a woman under the left arm, or, for a child, suspended from the neck by a linen cord. Linen was sacred because the body of Christ was buried in a linen shroud.

1. *p. 89;* see III, 180–1.
2. I, 316–17.
3. *pp. 89, 93;* see III, 182.

The Path of Right

My walk this day with God
My walk this day with Christ,
My walk this day with Spirit,
>The Threefold all-kindly:
>Hò! hò! hò! the Threefold all-kindly.

My shielding this day from ill,
My shielding this night from harm,
Hò! hò! both my soul and my body,
>Be by Father, by Son, by Holy Spirit:
>By Father, by Son, by Holy Spirit.

Be the Father shielding me,
Be the Son shielding me,
Be the Spirit shielding me,
>As Three and as One:
>Hò! hò! hò! as Three and as One.

III, 49

Journey Blessings

May God make safe to you each steep,
May God make open to you each pass,
May God make clear to you each road,
>And may He take you in the clasp of His own two hands.

III, 203

The Aiding

May Brigit shield me,
May Mary shield me,
May Michael shield me,
    On sea and on land:
        To shield me from all anguish
    On sea and on land,
        To shield me from all anguish.

May Father aid me,
May Son aid me,
May Spirit aid me,
    On sea and on land:
        In the shielding of the City everlasting
    On sea and on land,
        In the shielding of the City everlasting.

May the Three succor me,
May the Three follow me,
May the Three guide me,
    On sea and on land,
        To the Vine-garden of the godlike
    On sea and on land,
        To the Vine-garden of the godlike.

III, 175

The Prayer

I am praying and appealing to God,
The Son of Mary and the Spirit of truth,
To aid me in distress of sea and of land:
May the Three succor me, may the Three shield me,
 May the Three watch me by day and by night.

God and Jesus and the Spirit of cleansing
Be shielding me, be possessing me, be aiding me,
Be clearing my path and going before my soul
In hollow, on hill, on plain.
  On sea and land be the Three aiding me.

God and Jesus and the Holy Spirit
Be shielding and saving me,
As Three and as One,
By my knee, by my back, by my side,
 Each step of the stormy world.

  III, 173

The Pilgrims' Aiding

God be with thee in every pass,
Jesus be with thee on every hill,
Spirit be with thee on every stream,
 Headland and ridge and lawn;

Each sea and land, each moor and meadow,
Each lying down, each rising up,
In the trough of the waves, on the crest of the billows,
 Each step of the journey thou goest.

  III, 195

The Journey Blessing

Bless to me, O God,
    The earth beneath my foot,
Bless to me, O God,
    The path whereon I go;
Bless to me, O God,
    The thing of my desire;
        Thou Evermore of evermore,
    Bless Thou to me my rest.

Bless to me the thing
    Whereon is set my mind,
Bless to me the thing
    Whereon is set my love;
Bless to me the thing
    Whereon is set my hope;
        O Thou King of kings,
    Bless Thou to me mine eye!

III, 181

Journey Blessings

May God shield you on every steep,
May Christ keep you in every path,
May Spirit bathe you in every pass.

III, 203

The Journey Prayer

God, bless to me this day,
    God, bless to me this night;
Bless, O bless, Thou god of Grace,
    Each day and hour of my life;
Bless, O bless, Thou God of grace,
    Each day and hour of my life.

God, bless the pathway on which I go,
    God, bless the earth that is beneath my sole;
Bless, O God, and give to me Thy love,
    O God of gods, bless my rest and my repose;
Bless, O God, and give to me Thy love,
    And bless, O God of gods, my repose.

III, 179

Prayer

Relieve Thou, O God, each one
In suffering on land or sea,
In grief or wounded or weeping,
And lead them to the house of Thy peace
    This night.

I am weary, weak and cold,
I am weary of traveling land and sea,
I am weary of traversing moorland and billow,
Grant me peace in the nearness of Thy repose
    This night.

Beloved Father of my God,
  Accept the caring for my tears;
  I would wish reconcilement with Thee,
  Through the witness and the ransom
    Of Thy Son;

To be resting with Jesus
  In the dwelling of peace,
  In the paradise of gentleness,
  In the fairy-bower
    Of mercy.

III, 177

Be Thou a Smooth Way

Be Thou a smooth way before me,
Be Thou a guiding star above me,
Be Thou a keen eye behind me,
This day, this night, for ever.

I am weary, and I am forlorn,
Lead Thou me to the land of the angels;
Methinks it were time I went for a space
To the court of Christ, to the peace of heaven;

If only Thou, O God of life,
Be at peace with me, be my support,
Be to me as a star, be to me as a helm,
From my lying down in peace to my rising anew.

I, 171

Prayer for Traveling

Life be in my speech,
Sense in what I say.
The bloom of cherries on my lips,
Till I come back again.

The love Christ Jesus gave
Be filling every heart for me,
The love Christ Jesus gave
Filling me for every one.

Traversing corries, traversing forests,
Traversing valleys long and wild.
The fair white Mary still uphold me,
The Shepherd Jesu be my shield,
The fair white Mary still uphold me,
The Shepherd Jesu be my shield.

I, 317

The Gospel of the God of Life

The Gospel of the God of life
    To shelter thee, to aid thee;
Yea, the Gospel of beloved Christ
    The holy Gospel of the Lord;

To keep thee from all malice,
    From every dole and dolor;
To keep thee from all spite,
    From evil eye and anguish.

Thou shalt travel thither, thou shalt travel hither,
  Thou shalt travel hill and headland,
Thou shalt travel down, thou shalt travel up,
  Thou shalt travel ocean and narrow.

Christ Himself is shepherd over thee,
  Enfolding thee on every side;
He will not forsake thee hand or foot,
  Nor let evil come anigh thee.

III, 191

The Gospel of Christ

I set the keeping of Christ about thee,
I set the guarding of God with thee,
  To possess thee, to protect thee
  From drowning, from danger, from loss,
  From drowning, from danger, from loss.

The Gospel of the God of grace
  Be from thy summit to thy sole;
The Gospel of Christ, King of salvation,
  Be as a mantle to thy body,
  Be as a mantle to thy body.

Nor drowned be thou at sea,
  Nor slain be thou on land,
Nor o'erborne be thou by man,
  Nor undone be thou by woman,
  Nor undone be thou by woman!

III, 193

Prayers for Healing

PRAYERS AND INCANTATIONS for help in times of suffering and illness naturally played a very important part in the lives of the Hebrideans. They saw the universe around them as the creation of a God whom they addressed as "the Being of Life," and that in it were many gifts for their use in healing. We are today recovering an awareness of that world as the interest in natural healing and herbal medicine becomes increasingly popular, and its significance is appreciated. It seems an appropriate time to turn again to what we find in the *Carmina Gadelica*.

Because the saints were so much a living part of their world, they often associated particular plants not only with peculiar healing properties but also with the names of a popular saint. Thus, Saint John's wort was also known as Saint Columba's wort, since according to tradition, the saint always carried the plant on his person. To be effective, the plant had to be accidentally found, and then secretly secured under the left armpit, either in the bodices of the women or in the vests of the men. The joy of finding it was great, for it not only warded off death and the evil eye but brought peace and plenty to the house, and growth and fruitfulness in the field:

Saint John's wort, Saint John's wort,
Without search, without seeking!
Please God and Christ Jesus
This year I shall not die.

Many prayers for healing involved some simple ritual, such as this which Carmichael heard from a gillie and gamekeeper Willie Maclean, whom he described as sitting with his big Bible before him who told what he did when a mote goes into the eye—a common accident particularly when winnowing.

You drink a mouthful of water from a small basin and pray to the God of life to bring the mote out of the man's eye and to place it on your tongue. You put back the mouthful of water in the little basin in your hand time after time, until you get the mote on your tongue—three times in succession, according to the three persons of the Trinity. You draw up the water in name of Father, in name of Son, in name of Spirit, in name of the powerful Holy Trinity and say:

May the King of life be giving rest,
May the Christ of love be giving repose,
    May the Spirit Holy be giving strength,
May the eye be at peace.[1]

The blessing of water used in healing was always done rhythmically in honor of the three members of the Trinity, whom they addressed as "everlasting, kindly, wise." For the healing of a cataract on the eye (known as scale because it resembled a herring scale, and was feared since if it spread it would cover the eyeball and cause blindness), the custom was to take three blades of grass and dip them in a bowl of water. Then as they were drawn softly across the cataract and the speaker would "ask the everlasting Trinity of life to grant me my prayer if it be Their own will so to do, and if the asking be in accord with Their mind:

God the Father,
God the Son,
God the Spirit,
> For guidance and mercy and compassion.

The protecting presence of God, which is so strong an element in Celtic spirituality, comes into play forcefully in this area of healing. For the God who creates and sustains is above all present in times of difficulty, distress, old age:

> But Thou, O Christ, gentle Son Mary,
>> Thou Being Who puttest sap in wood,
> Pour Thy grace into the bones unfruitful,
>> Pour Thy light into the eyes of the blind!

> Pour Thy dew into the joints unpliant,
>> Pour Thy salve into the eye without light,
> Lead Thou my soul to the dwelling of the martyrs,
>> Sustain my feel to the home of the saints!

After all, Christ and his mother had walked the earth, and as they think back to the time of his earthly life, they pictured them in a Holy Land that had much about it of their own countryside:

Jesus and his Mother were walking by the side of a river in the Holy Land. And but that it was a gentle autumn evening, the sun about to sink in the depth of the ocean, scattering gold-yellow and gold-red upon the crests of the mountains and upon the surface of the waves. And in the meeting of day and night, what but a white-bellied salmon leaped with a great rush up the rough bed of the stream. Christ noticed that the salmon was wanting the sight of one eye, and He desired the Mary Mother to give the sight of eye to the salmon….

So Mary will also be included in the prayers for healing, and women will ask for her help "with the lips of her mouth and with the cords of her heart." Here once again we are faced with the totality of a world in which the past and the present, the natural and the human, are all bound together and all center on the Trinity who, together with Mary and the saints are so familiar and who hold out such assurance of life.

1. IV, 237–9

For the Healing of a Wound

In Christ the loving,
   The holy Blood of powers.

(*The name and designation of the person or animal is added.*)

Closed for thee thy wound,
   And congeal thy blood.
As Christ bled upon the cross,
   So closeth He thy wound for thee.

IV, 285

Prayer for Chest Constriction

Jesus Christ bade Simon Peter
    To fill His own people,
        To teach His own people,
    To shield His own people,
        To succor His own people,
To save His own people
From robbers, from betrayers.

    I am appealing to Thee,
    I am praying of Thee,
        Since Thou art the King of each good,
        Since Thou art the King of heaven,
            That Thou mayest lift each wasting,
    Each weariness and weakness,
        Each seizure and ailment,
    Each soreness and discomfort,
        Each malady and sickness
    That adheres to this maiden.

    I am praying of Thee keenly,
        I am calling on Thee straitly,
    That Thou mayest lift each stroke,
        Each injury and bane.

As severs flood from flood,
    As severs water from water,
As severs liquid from liquid
    Throughout the vastness of the watery ocean,

As sunders haze from haze,
As sunders mist from mist,
As sunders cloud from cloud
In the depth of the great stormy sky,

As scatter "òin" from "òin,"
As scatter birds from birds,
May the God of guidance scatter this night
Each ill and affection that was ever in thy flesh.

    It will cause them no harm,
        And it will cause good to thee, [to him]
    Thou dear Margaret Calder,
        Mine own sister.   [brother]

Prayer for Chest Disease

    The hands of God be round thee,
    The eye of God be over thee,
    The love of the King of the heavens
        Drain from thee thy pang.

    Away! Away! Away!
    Dumbly! Dumbly! Dumbly!
    Thy venom be in the ground,
        Thy pain be in the stone!

    II, 307

A Swollen Breast

The legend says that Mary and Jesus were walking together when Mary took Rose (erysipelas) in her breast, and she said to Jesus:

Behold, Son and Christ,
The breast of Thy Mother swollen,
Give Thou peace to the breast,
Subdue Thou the swelling;
> Give Thou peace to the breast,
> Subdue Thou the swelling.

Behold it thyself, Queen,
Since of thee the Son was born,
Appease thou the breast,
Subdue thou the swelling;
> Appease thou the breast,
> Subdue thou the swelling.

See Thou it, Jesu,
Since Thou art King of life,
Appease Thou the breast,
Subdue Thou the udder;
> Appease Thou the breast,
> Subdue Thou the udder.

I behold, said Christ,
And I do as is meet,
I give ease to the breast,
And rest to the udder;
> I give ease to the breast,
> And rest to the udder.

II, 3

For Swollen Breast

Extinction to thy microbe,
    Extinction to thy swelling,
Peace be to thy breast,
    The peace of the King of power.

Whiteness be to thy skin,
    Subsiding to thy swelling,
Wholeness to thy breast,
    Fullness to thy pap.

In the holy presence of the Father,
    In the holy presence of the Son,
In the holy presence of the Spirit,
    The holy presence of compassion.

IV, 195

For Rupture

O God of grace, satisfy my body;
O Christ of the Passion, satisfy my soul;
O Spirit of wisdom, vouchsafe me light,
    And restore to me repose.

Father of all life, strengthen my hand;
O Son of love, soothe Thou the pain;
O Spirit Holy, reduce the rupture,
    And . . .

II, 279

For Sprain

He Who so calmly rode
  The little ass fair of form,
Who healed each hurt and bloody wound
  That clave to the people of every age:

He made glad the sad and the outcast,
  He gave rest to the restless and the tired,
He made free the bond and the unruly,
  Each old and young in the land.

He opened the eyes of the blind,
  He awaked the step of the lame,
He loosed the tongue that was dumb,
  He gave life to him that was dead.

He stemmed the fierce-rushing blood,
  He took the keen prickle from the eye,
He drank the draught that was bitter,
  Trusting to the High Father of heaven.

He gave strength to Peter and Paul,
  He gave strength to the Mother of tears,
He gave strength to Brigit of the flocks,
  Each joint and bone and sinew.

IV, 209–11

Prayer for Sprain

Christ went out
In the morning early,
He found the legs of the horses
In fragments soft:
He put marrow to marrow,
He put pith to pith,
He put bone to bone,
He put membrane to membrane,
He put tendon to tendon,
He put blood to blood,
He put tallow to tallow,
He put flesh to flesh,
He put fat to fat,
He put skin to skin,
He put warm to warm,
He put cool to cool,
As the King of power healed that
It is in His nature to heal this,
If it be His own will to do it.

> Through the bosom of the Being of life,
> And of the Three of the Trinity.

II, 21

A Prayer for Succor

For the sake of Thine anguish and Thy tears,
    For the sake of Thy pain and Thy passion,
Good Son of Mary, be in peace with me
    And succor me at my death!

Thou are my precious Lord,
    Thou art my strong pillar,
Thou art the sustenance of my breast:
    Oh part Thou from me never!

For mine afflictions forsake me not,
    For my tears' sake do not leave me!
Jesu! Thou likeness of the sun,
    In the day of my need be near me!

Thou great Lord of the sun,
    In the day of my need be near me;
Thou great Being of the universe,
    Keep me in the surety of Thine arms!

Leave me not in dumbness,
    Dead in the wilderness;
Leave me not to my stumbling,
    For my trust is in Thee, my Savior!

Though I had no fire,
    Thy warmth did not fail me;
Though I had no clothing,
    Thy love did not forsake me.

Though I had no hearth,
    The cold did not numb me;
Though I knew not the ways,
    Thy knowledge was around me.

Though I had no bed,
    I lacked not for sleep,
For Christ's arm was my pillow,
    His eye supreme was my protection.

Though I was forlorn,
    Hunger came not near me,
For Christ's Body was my food,
    The Blood of Christ, it was my drink.

IV, 333–5

Saint Columba's Plant

I will pluck what I meet,
As in communion with my saint,
To stop the wiles of wily men,
    And the arts of foolish women.

I will pluck my Columba plant,
As a prayer to my King,
That mine be the power of Columba's plant,
    Over every one I see.

I will pluck the leaf above,
As ordained of the High King,
In name of the Three of glory,
    And of Mary, Mother of Christ.

II, 99

Saint John's Wort

Soothing and salving
With the wort of Columba,
Soothing and salving
   With the grace of the God of life.

Soothing and salving
With the wort of Columba,
Soothing and salving
   With the grace of the Christ of love.

Soothing and salving
With the wort of Columba,
Soothing and salving
   With the grace of the Holy Ghost.

Soothing and salving
With the wort of Columba,
Soothing and salving
   With the grace of the Three in One.

Soothing and salving
In the strength of the sweet kisses
From the mouth and the lips
   Of the Three element and kind.

IV, 211

Prayers for Protection

IN A LIFE which was full of danger and uncertainty prayers for protection were common and the shielding of God was seen as a very immediate reality. The ritual of encompassment (*caim*) which is referred to a number of times in this section brought a sense of security and assurance that God, the saints, and angels were called in to the aid of those in need. The *caim* was an imaginary circle which anyone in fear, danger, or distress made by stretching out the right hand with the forefinger extended and turning sunwise, as though on a pivot, so that the circle enclosed and accompanied the man or woman as they walked, and safeguarded them from all evil, within and without.[1]

1. III, 102.

The Three

The Three Who are over me,
The Three Who are below me,
The Three Who are above me here,
The Three Who are above me yonder;
The Three Who are in the earth,
The Three Who are in the air,
The Three Who are in the heaven,
    The Three Who are in the great pouring sea.

III, 93

Encompassment

The holy Apostles' guarding,
The gentle martyrs' guarding,
The nine angels' guarding,
    Be cherishing me, be aiding me.

The quiet Brigit's guarding,
The gentle Mary's guarding,
The warrior Michael's guarding,
    Be shielding me, be aiding me.

The God of the elements' guarding,
The loving Christ's guarding,
The Holy Spirit's guarding,
    Be cherishing me, be aiding me.

III, 107

Encompassing

The compassing of God be on thee,
    The compassing of the God of life.

The compassing of Christ be on thee,
    The compassing of the Christ of love.

The compassing of Spirit be on thee,
    The compassing of the Spirit of Grace.

The compassing of the Three be on thee,
    The compassing of the Three preserve thee,
    The compassing of the Three preserve thee.

III, 105

Encompassing

The compassing of God and His right hand
Be upon my form and upon my frame;
The compassing of the High King and the grace of the Trinity
Be upon me abiding ever eternally,
   Be upon me abiding ever eternally.

May the compassing of the Three shield me in my means,
The compassing of the Three shield me this day,
The compassing of the Three shield me this night
From hate, from harm, from act, from ill,
   From hate, from harm, from act, from ill.

III, 103

Jesus, the Encompasser

Jesu! Only-begotten Son and Lamb of God the Father,
Thou didst give the wine-blood of Thy body
        to buy me from the grave.
My Christ! my Christ! my shield, my encircler,
Each day, each night, each light, each dark;
    My Christ! my Christ! my shield, my encircler,
    Each day, each night, each light, each dark.

Be near me, uphold me, my treasure, my triumph,

In my lying, in my standing, in my watching, in my sleeping.

Jesu, Son of Mary! my helper, my encircler,
Jesu, Son of David! my strength everlasting;
    Jesu, Son of Mary! my helper, my encircler,
    Jesu, Son of David! my strength everlasting.

III, 77

The Homestead

O God, bless my homestead,
　　Bless Thou all therein.

O God, bless my kindred,
　　Bless Thou my substance.

O God, bless my words,
　　Bless Thou my converse.

O God, bless my errand,
　　Bless Thou my journey.

O God, lessen my sin,
　　Increase Thou my trust.

O God, ward from me distress,
　　Ward Thou from me misfortune.

O God, shield me from guilt,
　　Fill Thou me with joy.

And, O God, let naught to my body
That shall do harm to my soul
When I enter the fellowship
　　Of the great Son of Mary.

III, 359

Prayer

I am appealing to God,
    And to Mary the Mother of Christ,
To Paul and the Apostles twelve,
    To aid me and to shield me.

I am beseeching the Lord,
    And Mary ever a Virgin,
To succor me and to aid me
    From evil and evildoing.

May God be aiding me,
    May God be succoring me,
May God be aiding me
    When near the reefs.

May God safeguard me
    When among the lepers,
May God safeguard me
    When in narrow course.

The Son of God be shielding me from harm,
The Son of God be shielding me from ill,
The Son of God be shielding me from mishap,
The Son of God be shielding me this night.

The Son of God be shielding me with might,
The Son of God be shielding me with power;
Each one who is dealing with me aright,
    So may God deal with his soul.

May God free me from every wickedness,
May God free me from every entrapment,
May God free me from every gully,
    From every torturous road, from every slough.

May God open to me every pass,
Christ open to me every narrow way,
Each soul of holy man and woman in heaven
Be preparing for me my pathway.

May God lift me up from the state of death,
From the state of torments to the state of grace,
From the earthly state of the world below
To the holy state of the high heavens.

May the fragrant Father of heaven
Be taking charge of my soul,
With His loving arm about my body,
    Through each slumber and sleep of my life.

III, 99–101

Petition

O holy God of Truth,
O loving God of mercy,
Sign me from the spells,
Sign me from the charms.

Compassionate God of life,
Forgiveness to me give,
    In my wanton talk,
    In my lying oath,
    In my foolish deed,
    In my empty speech.

Compassionate God of life,
    Screen from me the bane of the silent women;
Compassionate God of life,
    Screen from me the bane of the wanton women;
Compassionate God of life,
    Screen from me the bane of the fairy women;
Compassionate God of life,
    Screen from me the bane of the false women.

    As Thou wast before
    At my life's beginning,
    Be Thou so again
        At my journey's end.

    As Thou wast besides
    At my soul's shaping,
    Father, be Thou too
        At my journey's close.

Be with me at each time,
Lying down and arising,
Be with me in sleep
　　Companioned by dear ones.

Be with me a-watching
Each evening and morning,
And allure me home
　　To the land of the saints.

III, 65–7

Charm for Fear by Night

God before me, God behind me,
God above me, God below me;
I on the path of God,
God upon my track.

　　Who is there on land?
　　Who is there on wave?
　　Who is there on billow?
　　Who is there by door-post?
　　Who is along with us?
　　　　God and Lord.

I am here abroad,
I am here in need,
I am here in pain,
I am here in straits,
I am here alone,
　　O God, aid me.

III, 319

Mary

 IN TALKING WITH CARMICHAEL, people would frequently interject "Mary Mother" or "O Mary of grace," an indication of their sense of ease and familiarity towards her. A Protestant woman, a crofter in Lochaber, addressing her grandchildren said "Be still, children, be quiet, you would cause the mild Mary of grace to sin!"[1]

A feast day of Mary is August 15. The people went early into the fields to pluck ears of corn to dry, grind and knead into a bannock which they roasted on a fire of rowan and shared between the whole family. They then walked sunwise round the fire and sang the "Peace of Mary Mother" who promised to shield them until the day of death.[2]

Carmichael seems to have been unaware that when he took down "Hail, Mary!"[3] this was not in fact true oral tradition but simply the Gaelic version of the Catholic hymn. However, since I feel that it stands in its own right, I have included it here.

1. III, 118.
2. *p. 117.*
3. *p. 129.*

The Feast Day of Mary

On the feast day of Mary the fragrant,
Mother of the Shepherd of the flocks,
I cut me a handful of the new corn,
I dried it gently in the sun,
I rubbed it sharply from the husk
    With mine own palms.

I ground it in a quern on Friday,
I baked it on a fan of sheep-skin,
I toasted it to a fire of rowan,
And I shared it round my people.

I went sunways round my dwelling,
In name of the Mary Mother,
Who promised to preserve me,
Who did preserve me,
And who will preserve me,
In peace, in flocks,
In righteousness of heart,

In labor, in love,
In wisdom, in mercy,
For the sake of Thy Passion.
Thou Christ of grace
Who till the day of my death
Wilt never forsake me!
    Oh, till the day of my death
    Wilt never forsake me!

I, 195–7

The Virgin

The Virgin was beheld approaching,
Christ so young on her breast,
Angels bowing lowly before them,
And the King of life was saying, 'Tis meet.

The Virgin of locks most glorious,
The Jesus more gleaming-white than snow,
Seraphs melodious singing their praise,
And the King of life was saying, 'Tis meet.

O Mary Mother of wondrous power,
Grant us the succor of thy strength,
Bless the provision, bless the board,
Bless the ear, the corn, the food.

The Virgin of mien most glorious,
The Jesus more gleaming-white than snow,
She like the moon in the hills arising,
He like the sun on the mountain-crests.

III, 115

The Virgin and Child

Behold the Virgin approaching,
Christ so young on her breast.

O Mary Virgin! and O Holy Son!
Bless ye the house and all therein.

Bless ye the food, bless ye the board,
Bless ye the corn, the flock and the store.

What time to us the quarter was scarce,
It is thou thyself, Virgin, who wast mother to us.

Thou art brighter than the waxing moon
Rising over the mountains.

Thou art brighter than the summer sun,
Under his fullness of joy.

Since the bard must not tarry,
Place ye alms in the bag with a blessing.

Servant am I of God the Son on the threshold,
For the sake of God, arise thyself and open to me.

I, 145

Praise of Mary

I say the prayer
That was given with anointing
To the Mary Mother
    Of joy;

Along with Pater and Credo,
The Prayer of Mary besides,
And the Prayer of God's Son
    Of the Passion;

To magnify thine own honor,
To magnify the glory of God's Son,
To magnify the greatness of the God
    Of grace.

Plead with thy gracious Son
That He make my prayer avail
My soul, and thereafter
    My body.

Thou Queen of the angels,
Thou Queen of the kingdom,
Thou Queen of the city
    Of glory:

Enfold me in every virtue,
Encompass me from every vice

. . . . .

Thou shining Mother of gentleness,
Thou glorious Mother of the stars,
Blessed hast thou been of every race
    And people.

O thou, alone praised, worthy of praise,
Make fervent prayer for me
With the Lord of the worlds,
    The God of life.

Thou Mary, gentle, fair, gracious,
I pray that thou forsake me not
In the sharp pang
    Of my death.

Shield of every dwelling, shield of every people
That are solely calling
On the gracious mercy
    Of thy dear Son:

Thou art the Queen-maiden of sweetness,
Thou art the Queen-maiden of faithfulness,
Thou art the Queen-maiden of peacefulness
    And of the peoples.

Thou art the well of compassion,
Thou art the root of consolations,
Thou art the living stream of the virgins
    And of them who bear child.

Thou art the tabernacle of Christ,
Thou art the mansion of Christ,
Thou art the ark of Christ—
    Of Him alone.

Thou art the Queen-maiden of the sea,
Thou art the Queen-maiden of the kingdom,
Thou art the Queen-maiden of the angels
    In effulgence.

Thou art the temple of the God of life,
Thou art the tabernacle of the God of life,
Thou art the mansion of the God of life
    And of the forlorn.

Thou art the river of grace,
Thou art the well-spring of salvation,
Thou art the garden and the paradise
    Of the virgins.

Thou art the star of morning,
Thou art the star of watching,
Thou art the star of the ocean
        Great.

Thou art the star of the earth,
Thou art the star of the kingdom,
Thou art the star of the Son of the Father
    Of glory.

Thou art the corn of the land,
Thou art the treasury of the sea,
The wished-for visitant of the homes
    Of the world.

Thou art the vessel of fullness,
Thou art the cup of wisdom,
Thou art the well-spring of health
    Of mankind.

Thou art the garden of virtues,
Thou art the mansion of gladness,
Thou art the Mother of sadness
    And of clemency.

Thou art the garden of apples,
Thou art the lull-song of the great folks,
Thou art the fulfillment of the world's desire
    In loveliness.

Thou art the sun of the heavens,
Thou art the moon of the skies,
Thou art the star and the path
    Of the wanderers.

Since thou art the full ocean
    Pilot me at sea;
Since thou art the dry shore,
    Save me upon land.

Since thou art the gem of the jewel,
Save me from fire and from water,
Save me from sky-hosts of evil
    And from fairy shafts.

There is none who utters my song
    Or puts it into use,
But Mary will show herself to him
    Three times before his death and his end.

III, 127–31

Prayer to Mary Mother

O Mary Maiden,
    Never was known
One who was placed
    'Neath thy generous care,

Who asked thy mercy,
    Who asked thy shielding,
Who asked thy succor
    With truthful heart,

Who found not thy solace,
    Who found not thy peace,
Who found not the succor
    For which he sought.

That gives unto me
    The hope excelling
That my tears and my prayer
    May find guest-room with thee.

My heart is content
    To kneel at thy footstool,
My heart is content
    In thy favor and hearing;

To come into thy presence,
    Beauteous one of smiles,
To come into thy presence,
    Beauteous one of women;

To come into thy presence,
    Queen-maiden of mankind,
To come into thy presence,
    Queen-maiden of the worlds;

To come into thy presence,
    O flower-garland of branches,
To come into thy presence,
    Bright garland of the heavens;

To come into thy presence,
    O Mother of the Lamb of Grace,
To come into thy presence,
    O Mother of the Paschal Lamb;

To come into thy presence,
    O river of seed,
To come into thy presence,
    O vessel of peace;

To come into thy presence,
    O fountain of healing,
To come into thy presence,
    O well-spring of grace;

To come into thy presence,
    Thou dwelling of meekness,
To come into thy presence,
    Thou home of peace;

To come into thy presence,
    Thou jewel of the clouds,
To come into thy presence.
    Thou jewel of the stars;

To come into thy presence,
  O Mother of black sorrow,
To come into thy presence,
  O Mother of the God of glory;

To come into thy presence,
  Thou Virgin of the lowly,
To come into thy presence,
  Thou Mother of Jesus Christ;

With lament and with sorrow,
  With prayer and supplication,
With grief and with weeping,
  With invoking and entreaty;

That thou mayest have me spared
  Shame and disgrace,
That thou mayest have me spared
  Flattery and scorn;

That thou mayest have me spared
  Misery and mourning,
That thou mayest have me spared
  Anguish eternal;

That thou mayest help my soul
  On the highway of the King,
That thou mayest help my soul
  On the roadway of peace;

That thou mayest help my soul
  In the doorway of mercy,
That thou mayest help my soul
  In the place of justice.

Since thou art the star of ocean,
    Pilot me at sea;
Since thou art the star of earth,
    Guide thou me on shore.

Since thou art the star of night,
    Lighten me in the darkness;
Since thou art the sun of day,
    Encompass me on land.

Since thou art the star of angels,
    Watch over me on earth;
Since thou art the star of paradise,
    Companion me to heaven.

Mayest thou shield me by night,
    Mayest thou shield me by day,
Mayest thou shield me by day and night,
    O bright and gracious Queen of heaven.

Grant me my prayer of love,
    Grant me my entreaty for shielding,
Grant me my supplication of pain
    Through the shed blood of the Son of thy
        breast.

Count me not as naught, O my God,
Count me not as naught, O my Christ,
Count me not as naught, O kind Spirit,
    And abandon me not to eternal loss.

III, 119–25

A Prayer

    O God,
In my deeds,
In my words,
In my wishes,
In my reason,
And in the fulfilling of my desires,
In my sleep,
In my dreams,
In my repose,
In my thoughts,
In my heart and soul always,
May the blessed Virgin Mary,
And the promised Branch of Glory dwell,
    Oh! in my heart and soul always,
    May the blessed Virgin Mary,
    And the fragrant Branch of glory dwell.

II, 27

Hail, Mary

Hail, Mary! hail, Mary!
    Queen of grace, Mother of mercy;
Hail, Mary, in manner surpassing,
    Fount of our health, source of our joy.

To thee we, night and day,
    Erring children of Adam and Eve,
Lift our voice in supplication,
    In groans and grief and tears.

Bestow upon us, thou Root of gladness,
    Since thou art the cup of generous graces,
The faith of John, and Peter, and Paul,
    With the wings of Ariel on the heights of the clouds.

Vouchsafe to us, thou golden branch,
    A mansion in the Realm of peace,
Rest from the perils and stress of waves,
    Beneath the shade of the fruit of thy womb, Jesu.

I, 109

Saints and Angels

THE STRONG SENSE of the closeness of eternity to the things of everyday comes across particularly strongly in the role that the angels and saints play in daily life. The phrase of a modern Welsh poet "keeping house among a cloud of witnesses"[1] catches something of the awareness that we find here. Heaven is never far away. In work and in sleep the heavenly powers lie close to hand. Thus a girl going out at night to the well would croon or lilt a hymn in the belief that the protecting arm of Mary and the saints would be shielding her from ill and mishap, natural or supernatural. (Brianag is the feminine of Brian, the god of light and leading among the Celts, so Brianag is light, guide, mother.)[2]

At night the soul-shrine would be sung asking for the guarding of the angels in sleep and shielding from harm. Should anything untoward happen either to themselves or to their flocks they would say that the cause was the "deadness of their hearts" or the "fewness of their prayers." At death they knew that the saints and angels would be waiting for them.[3]

Saint Bridget and her services in particular were very near to the hearts and lives of the people. In many ways she was as much if not more to them than Mary. Her day, February 1, was always a day of great rejoicing and jubilation. One of the most popular legends about her was that she was the serving-maid in the inn at Bethlehem who one day when two strangers asked for food and shelter offered them her own bannock of bread and stoup of water, all that she could give. Later to her amazement she found the bannock whole and the stoup full. Going to the door of the inn to gaze after them she saw a brilliant golden light under the stable door. She went in, and was in time to aid and minister to Mary and to receive the Child into her arms and to put three drops of water on his forehead in the name of the Trinity. She was therefore known as the aid-woman of Mary, the foster-mother of Christ. When a woman was in labor the midwife would go to the door of the house and with her hands on jambs softly beseech Bridget to come in.[4]

Saint Columba was always remembered on a Thursday, and the day looked on as a lucky day for any enterprise.[5]

The feast of Saint Michael, celebrated on September 29, used to be the most popular and imposing of the year. A cake (*struan*) was baked made of all the cereals grown on the farm during the year and a lamb killed, representing the fruits of the flocks. Great rituals accompanied the making of the *struan*. They were made for each individual member of the family or household, uniform in size but irregular in form: three-cornered, symbolic of the Trinity, five-cornered, symbolic of the Trinity with Mary and Joseph added, seven-cornered, for the mysteries, nine-cornered, for the archangels, or round as the symbol of eternity. On the morning of the feast everyone went to Mass taking their *struan* to be blessed by the priest and the service became the occasion of thanksgiving for the fruits of the fields and the flocks. Later in the day a procession on horseback if possible (it was permissible to "appropriate" a horse for the day) would circuit the burying ground, a great crowd starting from the east and following the course of the sun, the people in a column after the priests, singing the song of Michael victorious whose sword is keen to smite and whose arm is strong to save. The day ended with games and races, and with a ball in the evening. But by Alexander Carmichael's time all this had become obsolete. The devotion to Saint Michael however continued, and not least the concern with his duty of conveying the souls of the good to heaven after the soul has parted from the body and has been weighed.[6]

1. From "Pa Beth Yw Dyn?" by Waldo Williams in *Dail Pren*(Llandysul, Gomer Press, 1956), p. 67.
2. *p. 134;* see III, 168–9.
3. *p. 132;* see I, 90–1.
4. *pp. 133, 141–2.*.
5. *p. 135.*
6. *pp. 138–141;* see III, 138–43.

The Soul-Shrine

God, give charge to Thy blessed angels,
    To keep guard around this stead tonight,
A band sacred, strong, and steadfast,
    That will shield this soul-shrine from harm.

Safeguard Thou, God, this household tonight,
    Themselves and their means and their fame,
Deliver them from death, from distress, from harm,
    From the fruits of envy and of enmity.

Give Thou to us, O God of peace,
    Thankfulness despite our loss,
To obey Thy statutes here below,
    And to enjoy Thyself above.

    I, 91

Blessing of Brigit

I am under the shielding
    Of good Brigit each day;
I am under the shielding
    Of good Brigit each night.

I am under the keeping
    Of the Nurse of Mary,
Each early and late,
    Every dark, every light.

Brigit is my companion-woman,
    Brigit is my maker of song,
Brigit is my helping-woman,
    My choicest of women,
    my woman of guidance.

III, 161–3 (SHORTENED)

Blessing

Be each saint in heaven,
Each sainted woman in heaven,
Each angel in heaven
Stretching their arms for you,
Smoothing the way for you,
When you go thither
    Over the river hard to see;
Oh when you go thither home
    Over the river hard to see.

III, 203

Rune of the Well

The shelter of Mary Mother
Be nigh my hands and my feet
To go out to the well
> And to bring me safely home.
> And to bring me safely home.

May warrior Michael aid me,
May Brigit calm preserve me,
May sweet Brianag give me light,
> And Mary pure be near me,
> And Mary pure be near me.

III, 169

The Cross of the Saints and the Angels

The cross of the saints and of the angels with me
From the top of my face to the edge of my soles.

· · · · ·

O Michael mild, O Mary of glory,
O gentle Bride of the locks of gold,
Preserve ye me in the weakly body,
The three preserve me on the just path.
> Oh! three preserve me on the just path.

Preserve ye me in the soul-shrine poor,
Preserve ye me, and I so weak and naked,
Preserve ye me without offense on the way,
The preservation of the three upon me tonight.
> Oh! the three to shield me tonight.

I, 47

The Day of Saint Columba

Thursday of Columba benign,
Day to send sheep on prosperity,
Day to send cow on calf,
Day to put the web in the warp.

Day to put coracle on the brine,
Day to place the staff to the flag,
Day to bear, day to die,
Day to hunt the heights.

Day to put horses in harness,
Day to send herds to pasture,
Day to make prayer efficacious,
Day of my beloved, the Thursday,
    Day of my beloved, the Thursday.

I, 163

The Guardian Angel

Thou angel of God who hast charge of me
From the dear Father of mercifulness,
The shepherding kind of the fold of the saints
To make round about me this night;

Drive from me every temptation and danger,
Surround me on the sea of unrighteousness,
And in the narrows, crooks, and straits,
Keep thou my coracle, keep it always.

Be thou a bright flame before me,
Be thou a guiding star above me,
Be thou a smooth path below me,
And be a kindly shepherd behind me,
Today, tonight, and forever.

I am tired and I a stranger,
Lead thou me to the land of angels;
For me it is time to go home
To the court of Christ, to the peace of heaven.

I, 49

Angel Guardian

O Angel guardian of my right hand,
    Attend thou me this night,
Rescue thou me in the battling floods,
    Array me in thy linen, for I am naked,
    Succor me, for I am feeble and forlorn.

Steer thou my coracle in the crooked eddies,
    Guide thou my step in gap and in pit,
Guard thou me in the treacherous turnings,
    And save thou me from the scaith* of the wicked,
Save thou me from scaith this night.

Drive thou from me the taint of pollution,
    Encompass thou me till Doom from evil;
O kindly Angel of my right hand,
    Deliver thou me from the wicked this night,
    Deliver thou me this night!

III, 151

*scaith: injury, harm, or damage

Michael Militant

O Michael Militant,
    Thou king of the angels,
Shield thy people
    With the power of thy sword,
        Shield thy people
        With the power of thy sword.

Spread thy wing
    Over sea and land,
East and west,
    And shield us from the foe,
        East and west,
        And shield us from the foe.

Brighten thy feast
    From heaven above;
Be with us in the pilgrimage
    And in the twistings of the fight;
        Be with us in the pilgrimage
        And in the twistings of the fight.

Thou chief of chiefs,
    Thou chief of the needy,
Be with us in the journey
    And in the gleam of the river;
        Be with us in the journey
        And in the gleam of the river.

Thou chief of chiefs,
    Thou chief of angels,
Spread thy wing
    Over sea and land,
For thine is their fullness,
Thine is their fullness,
       Thine own is their fullness,
       Thine own is their fullness.

III, 145–7

Michael of the Angels

O Michael of the angels
And the righteous in heaven,
Shield thou my soul
    With the shade of thy wing;
Shield thou my soul
    On earth and in heaven;

From foes upon earth,
From foes beneath earth,
From foes in concealment
Protect and encircle
    My soul 'neath thy wing,
       Oh my soul with the shade of thy wing!

III, 149

Michael, the Victorious

Thou Michael the victorious,
I make my circuit under thy shield,
Thou Michael of the white steed,
And of the bright brilliant blades,
Conqueror of the dragon,
Be thou at my back,
Thou ranger of the heavens,
Thou warrior of the King of all,
O Michael the victorious,
My pride and my guide,
O Michael the victorious,
The glory of mine eye.

I make my circuit
In the fellowship of my saint,
On the machair,* on the meadow,
On the cold heathery hill;
Though I should travel ocean
And the hard globe of the world
No harm can e'er befall me
'Neath the shelter of thy shield;
O Michael the victorious,
Jewel of my heart,
O Michael the victorious,
God's shepherd thou art.

Be the sacred Three of Glory
Aye at peace with me,
With my horses, with my cattle,
With my woolly sheep in flocks.

With the crops growing in the field
Or ripening in the sheaf,
On the machair, on the moor,
In cole, in heap, or stack.
    Every thing on high or low,
    Every furnishing and flock,
    Belong to the holy Triune of glory,
    And to Michael the victorious.

    I, 209–11

*machair: level land, long stretches of sandy plains fringing
the Atlantic along the Outer Hebrides

Genealogy of Bride

The genealogy of the holy maiden Bride,
Radiant flame of gold, noble foster-mother of Christ.
Bride the daughter of Dugall the brown,
Son of Aodh, son of Art, son of Conn,
Son of Crearar, son of Cis, son of Carmac, son of Carruin.

Every day and every night
That I say the genealogy of Bride,
I shall not be killed, I shall not be harried,
I shall not be put in cell, I shall not be wounded,
Neither shall Christ leave me in forgetfulness.

No fire, no sun, no moon shall burn me,
No lake, no water, nor sea shall drown me,
No arrow of fairy nor dart of fay shall wound me,
And I under the protection of my Holy Mary,
And my gentle foster-mother is my beloved Bride.

    I, 175

Bride the Aid-Woman

There came to me assistance,
Mary fair and Bride;
As Anna bore Mary,
As Mary bore Christ,
As Eile* bore John the Baptist
Without flaw in him,
Aid thou me in mine unbearing,
    Aid me, O Bride!

As Christ was conceived of Mary
Full perfect on every hand,
Assist thou me, foster-mother,
The conception to bring from the bone;
And as thou didst aid the Virgin of joy,
Without gold, without corn, without kine,
Aid thou me, great is my sickness,
    Aid me, O Bride!

I, 177

*Eile: Elizabeth

Christmas Carols

ON CHRISTMAS EVE bands of young men went from house to house chanting Christmas songs. Each band selected a leader for their singing, called the song-man, and the others were the chorus-men. When they had finished their singing at a house two or three bannocks were handed out to them through a window. The song-man got half of every bannock, and the other half went to the chorus-men. Sometimes rituals were more elaborate and the members of the band were called "rejoicers." They would wear long white shirts for surplices and very tall white hats for miters. When they entered a house they took possession of a child, or else a lay figure was improvised. The assumed Christ would then be placed on a skin and carried three times round the fire sunwise while they sang the Christmas Hail.[1]

1. *pp. 145–8;* see I, 126.

The Child of Glory

The Child of glory
The Child of Mary,
Born in the stable
    The King of all,
Who came to the wilderness
And in our stead suffered;
Happy they are counted
    Who to Him are near.

When He Himself saw
That we were in travail,
Heaven opened graciously
    Over our head:
We beheld Christ,
The Spirit of truth,
The same drew us in
    'Neath the shield of His crown.

Strengthen our hope,
Enliven our joyance,
Keep us valiant,
    Faithful and near,
O light of our lantern,
Along with the virgins,
Singing in glory
    The anthem new.

III, 117

Christmas Carol

Hail King! hail King! blessed is He! blessed is He!
Hail King! hail King! blessed is He! blessed is He!
Hail King! hail King! blessed is He, the King of whom we sing,
    All hail! let there be joy!

This night is the eve of the great Nativity,
Born is the Son of Mary the Virgin,
The soles of His feet have reached the earth,
The Son of glory down from on high,
Heaven and earth glowed to Him,
    All hail! let there be joy!

The peace of earth to Him, the joy of heaven to Him, Behold
His feet have reached the world;
The homage of a King be His, the welcome of a Lamb be His,
King all victorious, Lamb all glorious,
Earth and ocean illumed to Him,
    All hail! let there be joy!

The mountains glowed to Him, the plains glowed to Him,
The voice of the waves with the song of the strand,
Announcing to us that Christ is born,
Son of the King of kings from the land of salvation;
Shone the sun on the mountains high to Him,
    All hail! let there be joy!

    Shone to Him the earth and sphere together,
    God the Lord has opened a Door;
    Son of Mary Virgin, hasten Thou to help me,
    Thou Christ of hope, Thou Door of joy,
    Golden Sun of hill and mountain,
        All hail! let there be joy!

    I, 133

Christmas Carol

This night is the long night,
> Hù ri vì hó hù,

It will snow and it will drift,
> Hù ri vì hó hù,

White snow there will be till day,
> Hù ri vì hó hù,

White moon there will be till morn,
> Hù ri vì hó hù.

This night is the eve of the Great Nativity,
> Hù ri vì hó hù,

This night is born Mary Virgin's Son,
> Hù ri vì hó hù,

This night is born Jesus, Son of the King of glory,
> Hù ri vì hó hù,

This night is born to us the root of our joy,
> Hù ri vì hó hù,

This night gleamed the sun of the mountains high,
> Hù ri vì hó hù,

This night gleamed sea and shore together,
> Hù ri vì hó hù,

This night was born Christ the King of greatness,
> Hù ri vì hó hù.

Ere it was heard that the Glory was come,
> Hù ri vì hó hù,

Heard was the wave upon the strand,
> Hù ri vì hó hù;

Ere 'twas heard that His foot had reached the earth,
> Hù ri vì hó hù.

> Heard was the song of the angels glorious,
> > Hù ri vì hó hù,

This night is the long night,
 Hù ri vì hó hù.

Glowed to Him wood and tree,
 Glowed to Him mount and sea,
Glowed to Him land and plain,
 When that His foot was come to earth.

III, 111–13

Christmas Chant

Hail King! hail King! blessed is He! blessed is He!
Hail King! hail King! blessed is He! blessed is He!
 Ho, hail! blessed the King!
 Ho, hi! let there be joy!

Prosperity be upon this dwelling,
On all that ye have heard and seen,
On the bare bright floor flags,
On the shapely standing stone staves,
 Hail King! hail King! blessed is He! blessed is He!

Bless this house and all that it contains,
From rafter and stone and beam;
Deliver it to God from pall to cover,
Be the healing of men therein,
 Hail King! hail King! blessed is He! blessed is He!

Be ye in lasting possession of the house,
Be ye healthy about the hearth,
Many be the ties and stakes in the homestead,
People dwelling on this foundation,
 Hail King! hail King! blessed is He! blessed is He!

Offer to the Being from found to cover,
Include stave and stone and beam;
Offer again both rods and cloth,
Be health to the people therein,
> Hail King! hail King! blessed is He! blessed is He!
> Hail King! hail King! blessed is He! blessed is He!
> > Ho, hail! blessed the King!
> > Let there be joy!

Blessed the King,
Without beginning, without ending,
To everlasting, to eternity,
> Every generation for aye,
> Ho! hi! let there be joy!

I, 135–7

Hey the Gift

Hey the Gift, ho the Gift,
Hey the Gift on the living.

The fair Mary went upon her knee,
It was the King of glory who was on her breast.

To tell to us that Christ is born,
The King of kings of the land of salvation

I see the hills, I see the strand,
I see the host upon the wing.

I see angels on clouds,
Coming with speech and friendship to us.

I, 139

Sun and Moon

MEN AND WOMEN saluted the morning sun and the new moon. They hailed the morning sun as they would a great person come back to their land, and the new moon, "the great lamp of grace," with joyous acclaim. As Isabel MacNeill of Barra told Carmichael:

> In my father's time there was not a man in Barra but would take off his head-covering to the white sun of the day, nor a woman in Barra but would incline her body to the white moon of the night....I think myself that it is a matter for thankfulness, the golden-bright sun of virtues giving us warmth and light by day, and the white moon of the seasons giving us guidance and leading by night.[1]

When the sun rose on the tops of the peaks an old man in Arasaig would put off his head-covering and would bow down his head, giving glory to the great God of life for the glory of the sun and for the goodness of its light to the children of men and to the animals of the world. When the sun set in the western ocean the old man would again take off his head-covering and he would bow his head to the ground and say:

> I am in hope, in its proper time,
> That the great and gracious God
> Will not put out for me the light of grace
> Even as thou dost leave me this night.[2]

But if the sun was to them a matter of great awe, they looked on the moon as a friend of great love, who guided their course on land and sea, and their path wherever they went. For a seafaring people the light and guidance of the moon could well be a matter of life and death when they had to thread their way through intricate reefs and rocks on a moonless night. This is one of the reasons for the many hymns addressed to the gracious luminary of the night.

1. III, 287.
2. III, 309.

Sun

The eye of the great God,
The eye of the God of glory,
The eye of the King of hosts,
The eye of the King of the living,
    Pouring upon us
        At each time and season,
    Pouring upon us
        Gently and generously.

Glory to thee,
    Thou glorious sun.

Glory to thee, thou sun,
    Face of the God of life.

III, 307

The Sun

Hail to thee, thou sun of the seasons,
    As thou traversest the skies aloft;
Thy steps are strong on the wing of the heavens,
    Thou art the glorious mother of the stars.

Thou liest down in the destructive ocean
    Without impairment and without fear;
Thou risest up on the peaceful wave-crest
    Like a queenly maiden in bloom.

III, 311

God of the Moon

God of the moon, God of the sun,
God of the globe, God of the stars,
God of the waters, the land, and the skies,
Who ordained to us the King of promise.

It was Mary fair who went upon her knee,
It was the King of life who went upon her lap,
Darkness and tears were set behind,
And the star of guidance went up early.

Illumed the land, illumed the world,
Illumed doldrum and current,
Grief was laid and joy was raised,
Music was set up with harp and pedal-harp.

II, 167

The New Moon

She of my love is the new moon,
    The King of all creatures blessing her;
Be mine a good purpose
    Towards each creature of creation.

      Holy be each thing
        Which she illumines;
      Kindly be each deed
        Which she reveals.

      Be her guidance on land
        With all beset ones;
      Be her guidance on the sea
        With all distressed ones.

      May the moon of moons
        Be coming through thick clouds
      On me and on every mortal
        Who is coming through affliction.

      May the virgin of my love
        Be coming through dense dark clouds
          To me and to each one
        Who is in tribulation.

      May the King of grace
        Be helping my hand
      Now and for ever
        Till my resurrection day.

III, 299

The New Moon

Hail to thee, thou new moon,
  Guiding jewel of gentleness!
I am bending to thee my knee,
  I am offering thee my love.

I am bending to thee my knee,
  I am giving thee my hand,
I am lifting to thee mine eye,
  O new moon of the seasons.

Hail to thee, thou new moon,
  Joyful maiden of my love!
Hail to thee, thou new moon,
  Joyful maiden of the graces!

Thou art traveling in thy course,
  Thou art steering the full tides;
Thou art illuming to us thy face,
  O new moon of the seasons

Thou queen-maiden of guidance,
  Thou queen-maiden of good fortune,
Thou queen-maiden my beloved,
  Thou new moon of the seasons!

III, 285

New Moon

May thy light be fair to me!
May thy course be smooth to me!
If good to me is thy beginning,
Seven times better be thine end,
    Thou fair moon of the seasons,
    Thou great lamp of grace!

He Who created thee
    Created me likewise;
He Who gave thee weight and light
    Gave to me life and death,
    And the joy of the seven satisfactions,
    Thou lamp of grace,
    Thou fair moon of the seasons.

III, 305

New Moon

Hail to thee, thou new moon,
    Beauteous guidant of the sky;
Hail to thee, thou new moon,
    Beauteous fair one of grace.

Hail to thee, thou new moon,
    Beauteous guidant of the stars;
Hail to thee, thou new moon,
    Beauteous loved one of my heart.

Hail to thee, thou new moon,
  Beauteous guidant of the clouds;
Hail to thee, thou new moon,
  Beauteous dear one of the heavens!

III, 275–7

New Moon

There, there, the new moon!
  The King of life making her bright for us;
Be mine a good intent
  Towards all who look on her.

Be mine eye upward
  To the gracious Father of blessings,
And be my heart below
  To the dear Christ Who purchased me.

Be my knee bent down
  To the queen of loveliness;
Be my voice raised up
  To Him Who made and blessed her.

III, 297

The New Moon

In the name of the Holy Spirit of grace,
In the name of the Father of the City of peace,
In the name of Jesus who took death off us,
Oh! in the name of the Three who shield us in every need,
If well thou hast found us tonight,
Seven times better mayest thou leave us without harm,
    Thou bright white Moon of the seasons,
    Bright white Moon of the seasons.

      May thy laying luster leave us
          Seven times still more blest.

          O moon so fair,
          May it be so,
          As seasons come,
          And seasons go.

I, 123

Invocations and Good Wishes

Prayer

The love of the Mary Mother be thine,
The love of Brigit of flocks be thine,
The love of Michael victorious be thine,
    With their arm each hour surrounding thee.

The great bounty of the sea be thine,
The great bounty of earth be thine,
The great bounty of heaven be thine,
    Thy life be hale and fruitful.

The mild grace of the Father be thine,
The loving grace of the Son be thine,
The loving grace of the Spirit be thine,
    Laying thee with the graces.

III, 243

Good Wish

The good of eye be thine,
The good of liking be thine,
   The good of my heart's desire.

The good of sons be thine,
The good of daughters be thine,
   The good of the sap of my sense.

The good of sea be thine,
The good of land be thine,
   The good of the Prince of heaven.

III, 239

Prayer

Each day be glad to thee,
No day be sad to thee,
   Life rich and satisfying.

Plenty be on thy course,
A son be on thy coming,
   A daughter on thine arriving.

The strong help of the serpent be thine,
The strong help of fire be thine,
   The strong help of the graces.

The love-death of joy be thine,
The love-death of Mary be thine,
   The loving arm of thy Savior.

III, 235

Prayer

I pray for thee a joyous life,
   Honor, estate and good repute,
No sigh from thy breast,
   No tear from thine eye.

No hindrance on thy path,
   No shadow on thy face,
Until thou lie down in that mansion,
   In the arms of Christ benign.

III, 239

God Guide Me

God guide me with Thy wisdom,
God chastise me with Thy justice,
God help me with Thy mercy,
God protect me with Thy Strength.

God fill me with Thy fullness,
God shield me with Thy shade,
God fill me with Thy grace,
For the sake of Thine Anointed Son.

Jesu Christ of the seed of David
Visiting One of the Temple,
Sacrificial Lamb of the Garden,
Who died for me.

    I, 65

Desires

May I speak each day according to Thy justice
Each day may I show Thy chastening, O God;
May I speak each day according to Thy wisdom,
Each day and night may I be at peace with Thee.

Each day may I count the causes of Thy mercy,
May I each day give heed to Thy laws;
Each day may I compose to Thee a song,
May I harp each day Thy praise, O God.

May I each day give love to Thee, Jesu,
Each night may I do the same;
Each day and night, dark and light,
May I laud Thy goodness to me, O God.

    I, 51

Good Wish

Wisdom of serpent be thine,
Wisdom of raven be thine,
    Wisdom of valiant eagle.

Voice of swan be thine,
Voice of honey be thine,
    Voice of the son of the stars.

Bounty of sea be thine,
Bounty of land be thine,
    Bounty of the Father of heaven.

    III, 241

Good Wish

The arm of Mary Mother be thine,
The arm of Brigit of flocks be thine,
The arm of Michael victorious be thine,
    To save thee from all sorrow.

The arm of Apostle John be thine,
The arm of Apostle Paul be thine,
The arm of Apostle Peter be thine,
    To guard thee from all mischief.

The arm of the God of life be thine,
The arm of Christ the loving be thine,
The arm of the Spirit Holy be thine,
    To shield thee and surround thee.

    III, 245

Grace

Grace of love be thine,
Grace of floor be thine,
Grace of castle be thine,
Grace of court be thine,
    Grace and pride of homeland be thine

The guard of the God of life be thine,
The guard of the loving Christ be thine,
The guard of the Holy Spirit be thine,

To cherish thee,
To aid thee,
To enfold thee.

The Three be about thy head,
The Three be about thy breast,
The Three be about thy body
    Each night and each day,
In the encompassment of the Three
    Throughout thy life long.

III, 229

The Gifts of the Three

Spirit, give me of Thine abundance,
Father, give me of Thy wisdom,
Son, give me in my need,
    Jesus beneath the shelter of Thy shield.

I lie down tonight,
With the Triune of my strength,
With the Father, with Jesus,
    With the Spirit of might.

I, 75

Short Blessings

The grace of God be with you,
    The grace of Christ be with you,
The grace of Spirit be with you
    And with your children,
        For an hour, forever, for eternity.

    III, 21

God's blessing be yours,
    And well may it befall you;
Christ's blessing be yours,
    And well be you entreated;
Spirit's blessing be yours,
    And well spend you your lives,
        Each day that you rise up,
           Each night that you lie down.

    III, 211

May the everlasting Father Himself take you
    In His own generous clasp,
    In His own generous arm.

    III, 903

God's grace distill on you,
Christ's grace distill on you,
Spirit's grace distill on you
    Each day and each night
        Of your portion in the world;
    Oh each day and each night
        Of your portion in the world.

III, 211

The blessing of God and the Lord be yours,
The blessing of the perfect Spirit be yours,
The blessing of the Three be pouring for you
    Mildly and generously,
    Mildly and generously.

III, 201

The guarding of the God of life be on you,
The guarding of loving Christ be on you,
The guarding of Holy Spirit be on you
    Every night of your lives,
To aid you and enfold you
    Each day and night of your lives.

III, 207

May the Father take you
    In His fragrant clasp of love,
When you go across the flooding streams
    And the black river of death.

III, 203

May God shield you on every steep,
May Christ aid you on every path,
May Spirit fill you on every slope,
    On hill and on plain.

    III, 209

May the King shield you in the valleys,
May Christ aid you on the mountains
May Spirit bathe you on the slopes,
    In hollow, on hill, on plain,
    Mountain, valley and plain.

    III, 209

May God's blessing be yours,
    And well may it befall you.

    III, 205

My own blessing be with you,
The blessing of God be with you,
The blessing of saints be with you
    And the peace of the life eternal,
    Unto the peace of the life eternal.

    III, 207

The love and affection of the angels be to you,
The love and affection of the saints be to you,
The love and affection of heaven be to you,
    To guard you and to cherish you.

    III, 207

The love and affection of heaven be to you,
The love and affection of the saints be to you,
The love and affection of the angels be to you,
The love and affection of the sun be to you,
The love and affection of the moon be to you,
     Each day and night of your lives,
          To keep you from haters, to keep you from harmers,
               to keep you from oppressors.

III, 209

The shape of Christ be towards me,
The shape of Christ be to me,
The shape of Christ be before me,
The shape of Christ be behind me,
The shape of Christ be over me,
The shape of Christ be under me,
The shape of Christ be with me,
The shape of Christ be around me,
On Monday and on Sunday;
     The shape of Christ be around me,
     On Monday and on Sunday.

III, 209

The eye of the great God be upon you,
The eye of the God of glory be on you,
The eye of the Son of Mary Virgin be on you,
The eye of the Spirit mild be on you,
     To aid you and to shepherd you;
Oh the kindly eye of the Three be on you,
     To aid you and to shepherd you.

III, 201

The peace of God be with you,
The peace of Christ be with you,
The peace of Spirit be with you
    And with your children,
From the day that we have here today
    To the day of the end of your lives,
    Until the day of the end of your lives.

III, 209

Fragment

As it was,
As it is,
As it shall be
Evermore,
O Thou Triune
Of grace!
With the ebb,
With the flow
O Thou Triune
Of grace!
With the ebb,
With the flow.

II, 217

Alphabetical Index of First Lines

A small drop of water *64*
As it was *168*

Be Christ's cross on your new
    dwelling *76*
Be each saint in heaven *133*
Be the great God between thy two
    shoulders *81*
Be this soul on Thine arm,
    O Christ *66*
Be Thou a smooth way
    before me *91*
Be with me, O God, at breaking
    of bread *80*
Behold, Son and Christ *100*
Behold the Virgin
    approaching *119*
Bless, O Chief of generous chiefs *46*
Bless, O God, my little cow *46*
Bless, O God, the fire *75*
Bless, O Threefold true and
    bountiful *26*
Bless to me, O God *6, 14, 89*
Bless to me, O God, the moon that
    is above me *8*

Christ went out *103*
Closed to you be every pit *27*
Come, Brendan, from the ocean *43*
Come, Mary, and milk my cow *44*
Come, thou Calum Cille kindly *45*

Each day be glad to thee *159*
Extinction to thy microbe *101*

Father, bless me in my body *11*
For the sake of Thine anguish and
    Thy tears *104*

Give the milk, my treasure! *42*
Give Thou to me, O God *70*
Give us, O God, of the morning
    meal *79*
Go shorn and come woolly *25*
God be with thee in every pass *88*
God before me, God behind me *115*
God bless the house *75*
God, bless the world and all
    that is therein *77*
God, bless Thou Thyself
    my reaping *23*
God, bless to me this day *90*
God, give charge to Thy blessed
    angels *132*
God guide me with Thy
    wisdom *160*
God of the moon,
    God of the sun *151*
God, omit not this woman from
    Thy covenant *69*
God the Father all-powerful,
    benign *32*

God to enfold me *20*
God with me lying down *12*
God's blessing be yours *164*
God's grace distill on you *165*
Grace of love be thine *162*

Hail King! hail King! blessed is He!
  blessed is He! *145, 147*
Hail, Mary! hail, Mary! *129*
Hail to thee, thou new moon *153,
  154*
Hail to thee, thou sun of the
  seasons *151*
He Who so calmly rode *102*
HELMSMAN   Blest be the boat *33*
Hey the Gift, ho the Gift *148*

I am appealing to God *112*
I am bending my knee *7*
I am going home with thee *73*
I am lying down tonight
  as beseems *54*
I am now going into the sleep *51*
I am placing my soul and
  my body *52, 60*
I am praying and appealing
  to God *88*
I am under the shielding *133*
I believe, O God of all gods *1*
I lie down this night with God *58*
I lie down tonight *55*
I lie in my bed *53*
I pray for thee a joyous life *159*
I say the prayer *120*
I set the keeping of Christ
  about thee *93*
I will build the hearth *40*
I will go out to sow the seed *24*
I will kindle my fire this
  morning *38*
I will place this flock before me *31*
I will pluck what I meet *105*
I will raise the hearth-fire *39*
In Christ the loving *97*
In name of Father *19, 63*
In name of God *65*
In the name of the Holy Spirit
  of grace *156*

In name of the Lord Jesus *57*
In Thy name, O Jesu Who wast
  crucified *56*
It were as easy for Jesu *5*

Jesu! Only-begotten Son and Lamb
  of God the Father *110*
Jesus Christ bade Simon Peter *98*
Jesus, Thou Son of Mary, I call on
  Thy name *72*

Life be in my speech *92*

May Brigit shield me *87*
May God make safe to you
  each steep *86*
May God shield you on every
  steep *89, 166*
May God's blessing be yours *166*
May I speak each day according to
  Thy justice *160*
May the everlasting Father Himself
  take you *164*
May the Father take you *165*
May the herding of Columba *28*
May the King shield you
  in the valleys *166*
May the Light of lights come *52*
May thy light be fair to me! *154*
My God and my Chief *9*
My own blessing be with you *166*
My walk this day with God *86*
My warp shall be very even *47*

O Angel guardian of my right
  hand *137*
O Being of life! *17*
O God *128*
O God, bless my homestead *111*
O God, give me of Thy wisdom *67*
O God of grace *101*
O God of life, darken not to me
  Thy light *51*
O God, who broughtest me from
  the rest of last night *20*
O holy God of Truth *114*
O Jesu! tonight *59*
O Jesu without sin *56*
O Mary Maiden *124*

O Michael Militant *138*
O Michael of the angels *139*
On Ash Eve *48*
On the feast day of Mary
   the fragrant *117*

Pastures smooth, long, and
   spreading *30*
Peace between neighbors *78*
Pray I this day my prayer to Thee,
   O God *10*

Relieve Thou, O God, each one *90*

She of my love is the new moon *152*
Since Thou Christ it was who didst
   buy the soul *66*
Soothing and salving *106*
Spirit, give me of Thine
   abundance *163*

Teat of Mary *41*
Thanks be to Thee, Jesus Christ *16*
Thanks be to Thee, O God *80*
Thanks to Thee ever,
   O gentle Christ *15*
Thanks to Thee, God *18*
Thanks to Thee, O God, that I have
   risen today *18*
The arm of Mary Mother
   be thine *161*
The benison of God be to thee *83*
The blessing of God and the Lord
   be yours *165*
The cattle are today going
   a-flitting *29*
The Child of glory *144*
The compassing of God and
   His right hand *109*
The compassing of God be
   on thee *108*
The cross of the saints and of the
   angels with me *134*
The day of light has come
   upon us *34*
The eye of the great God *150*
The eye of the great God be
   upon you *167*

The genealogy of the holy maiden
   Bride *141*
The good of eye be thine *158*
The Gospel of the God of life *92*
The grace of God be with you *164*
The guarding of the God of life
   be on you *165*
The hands of God be round thee *99*
The holy Apostles' guarding *108*
The joy of God be in thy face *82*
The love and affection of heaven
   be to you *167*
The love and affection of the angels
   be to you *166*
The love of the Mary Mother
   be thine *157*
The night the Herdsman
   was out *28*
The peace of God be with you *168*
The peace of God, the peace
   of men *78*
The sacred Three *40*
The shape of Christ be towards
   me *167*
The shelter of Mary Mother *134*
The Three Who are over me *107*
The Virgin was beheld
   approaching *118*
There came to me assistance *142*
There, there, the new moon! *155*
This night is the long night *146*
Thou angel of God who hast charge
   of me *136*
Thou goest home this night to thy
   home of winter *68*
Thou great God, grant me
   Thy light *58*
Thou King of moon and sun *14*
Thou Michael the victorious *140*
Thursday of Columba benign *135*

Where thou shalt bring the crown
   of thy head *84*
Wisdom of serpent be thine *161*